Britain's Relative Economic Performance, 1870–1999

Britain's Relative Economic Performance, 1870–1999

NICHOLAS CRAFTS

The Institute of Economic Affairs

First published in Great Britain in 2002 by
The Institute of Economic Affairs
2 Lord North Street
Westminster
London SW1P 3LB
in association with Profile Books Ltd

A CIP catalogue record for this book is available from the British Library.

ISBN 0 255 36524 1

Many IEA publications are translated into languages other than English or are
reprinted. Permission to translate or to reprint should be sought from the
General Director at the address above.

Typeset in Stone by MacGuru
info@macguru.org.uk

Printed and bound in Great Britain by Hobbs the Printers

CONTENTS

THE AUTHOR

Nicholas Crafts has been Professor of Economic History at the London School of Economics since 1995. Previously he was Fellow and Praelector in Economics at University College, Oxford (1977–86) and Professor of Economic History at the University of Warwick (1988–95).

He was born in 1949 and educated at Brunts Grammar School, Mansfield, and Trinity College, Cambridge. His publications include *Britain's Relative Economic Decline, 1870–1995* (1997), and articles in many journals including *Economic History Review, Economic Journal, Journal of Economic History* and *Journal of Economic Perspectives*. He is the author of *Globalisation and Growth in the 20th Century*, IMF Working Paper No. 00/44 (2000). He is Managing Editor of the *Economic History Review* and is a Fellow of the British Academy (elected 1992).

For the IEA, Professor Crafts has previously contributed *Can De-Industrialisation Seriously Damage Your Wealth?* (Hobart Paper No. 120, 1993) and *The Conservative Government's Economic Record* (Occasional Paper 104, 1998).

FOREWORD

Professor Nicholas Crafts presents a remarkable account of Britain's economic performance in the last 125 years. The economy's output per head has increased by more than 500 per cent, and this has enabled material living standards to rise about six times. What matters especially in the personal lives of families is that someone born in 1870 could expect to live to be 44 while a child born in 1997 could expect to live to be 77. Today's children can reasonably hope to see their grandchildren grow up and begin their careers, while our Victorian predecessors were fortunate if they survived until their children reached adulthood. The near-doubling of life expectations means that, for the great majority, there are fewer years of debilitating illness and far less suffering from ill health.

This has actually produced a considerable equalisation of personal welfare. Oxford and Cambridge graduates who went on to become country clergymen have always appeared to live into their seventies or eighties, and in 1870 the wealthy would have expected to live for many more years than the poor. Now, in the 21st century, life expectation in general exceeds 70. Nick Crafts estimates that the welfare gains from these improvements are comparable to those from the six-times rise in average material living standards. But both have been achieved, so where is Britain's *decline*, which is the subject of his brilliant paper? It is, of course, Britain's *comparative decline* in relation to the world's leading economies which he documents and analyses.

He offers a plethora of data of the most interesting kinds. As one of the world's most widely respected economic historians, he presents the best available data at every stage, and he warns us of their imperfections. As an economic historian who is also an economist, he draws on many previous studies of the British economy and its strengths and weaknesses, and presents the salient features of each.

In 1870 Britain's real output per head was greater than the USA's and that of every European economy: it was only exceeded by Australia's. By 1913 Britain had also been overtaken by the USA and New Zealand; but its output per head was still the fourth highest in the world. By 1950, after recovery from World War II, Britain had also been overtaken by Canada, and in Europe by Switzerland and Denmark. It was still 30 per cent ahead of the Six who were about to sign the Treaty of Rome, whom Britain could disregard in the knowledge that their economies were chronically weak, and that little would therefore come of their European project. Over the next two decades, the so-called Golden Age, Britain was overtaken by five of the six founder members of the EEC, together with Sweden, and by 1999, where Crafts' study terminates, Britain also ranked below Singapore, Hong Kong and Japan in Asia, and Norway, Ireland and Austria in Europe. In 1950 output per head was twice as great in Britain as in the Irish Republic. By 1999 Ireland had become a 'Celtic Tiger', and moved 7 per cent ahead of Britain. A citizen of Northern Ireland who votes to join the South in a future referendum will now be voting to unite with an economy which enjoys higher living standards and lower taxation.

However, British progress has never ceased, and its rate and extent would have astounded our predecessors. Nick Crafts remarks that living standards have risen 'by far more than would have been thought possible in earlier centuries'. In May 1822 David Ricardo, a founder of what Thomas Carlyle described as 'the Dismal Science', told the House of Commons:

> were the corn laws once got rid of, and our general policy in these subjects thoroughly revised, this would be the cheapest country in the world; and instead of our complaining that capital was withdrawn from us, we should find that capital would come hither from all corners of the civilized world ... England would be the cheapest country in which a man could live; and it would rise to a state of prosperity, in regard to population and riches, of which, perhaps, the imagination of honorary members could at present form no idea.[1]

Free trade actually became British policy in 1846, and the additional competition it fostered, together with the impact of cheap food and raw materials, helped Britain to achieve the world's highest output per head (Australia apart) in 1870.

Nick Crafts regards the subsequent overtaking of Britain by the USA in the decades before World War I as an inevitable consequence of the vast advantages in raw materials per head which it enjoyed. Until 1914, the British economy benefited from intense competition between many thousand entrepreneurs, with others ready to take their places if they failed. The Treasury had no professional economic advisers but it developed three rules to protect the country from rogue Chancellors.[2] Keeping the budget

---

1   Piero Sraffa (ed.), *The Works and Correspondence of David Ricardo*, Cambridge University Press, Cambridge, 1951–73, vol. V, pp. 187–8.
2   See George Peden in B. Corry (ed.), *Unemployment and the Economists*, Edward Elgar, Cheltenham, 1996, p. 76.

continually balanced ensured that additional public expenditure could only be proposed by Chancellors prepared to raise the potentially unpopular taxation required to finance it. Adherence to the gold standard protected the country from Chancellors who countenanced inflation, and Ricardo's free trade kept British industry and commerce internationally efficient.

Nick Crafts believes that Britain's serious errors began in the 1930s with the adoption of tariffs. These were compounded by the widespread dilution of competition in the 1950s, 1960s and 1970s, when Britain could have grown 1 per cent per annum faster and most of the overtaking by others occurred. There was no competition at all in the newly nationalised industries, while in the private sector inefficient companies were not allowed to fail. Nick Crafts diagnoses 'agency problems' as a key to the greatest weaknesses in the economy. Those who actually ran companies became distant and almost uncontrolled agents of their owners. Managements went their own way, and governments of both colours presided over industrial policies whereby ministers believed they were picking winners, while in reality disastrous managements were picking ministers. It is a fundamental element in Nick Crafts' argument, to which he returns again and again, that increased competition and not 'industrial policy' was actually the solution to the agency problems that bedevilled the British economy.

There were vast changes in the 1980s and 1990s. Competition was extended through privatisation. The DTI was deprived of money so it ceased to be able to fund losers. 'Big Bang' eliminated fixed margins in the City of London, and there was an abrupt end to the culture of so-called Three-Six-Three banking (where all depositors received 3 per cent, all borrowers paid 6 per cent and managers were free for golf by 3 p.m.). The European Single

Market and tougher competition law undermined price fixing and feather-bedding in a widening range of industries. The consequent microeconomic transformation of British industry and commerce removed many of the weaknesses that had led to comparative underperformance in the 1960s and 1970s.

Nick Crafts has no table which documents comparative international output per head between 1980 and 1999; but he makes it extremely clear that this was not a period in which Britain regained any of its competitive losses of the previous decades. Comparative decline was merely arrested: broadly speaking, after 1980, Britain advanced at about the same pace as other leading economies, whereas previously it was being overtaken by country after country.

Hopes of catch-up for Britain lie in the future. Nick Crafts believes that the IT revolution, which has been led by the United States, now has the potential to raise growth rates by perhaps 0.5 per cent per annum. Britain and Sweden, which share the advantage of English as a business language, are immeasurably better placed to exploit this than France, Germany, Italy and Spain. That is largely speculation.

Nick Crafts has no detectable bias, nor have the data. Professor Robin Matthews once remarked that no one studying the macroeconomic data of the British economy would detect from such statistics alone the colour of the government in power. There was political continuity in the policy errors of the 1950s, 1960s and 1970s, and there appears to be similar continuity in the competition-oriented policies that began to be adopted after 1979, and which have mainly been continued since the 1997 change of government. Gordon Brown has indeed almost resurrected the Treasury's three classical pillars of policy. His 'golden rule' comes close to the former balanced-budget objective. His monetary policy committee nearly entails gold standard discipline, and Britain is on the free trade side in every EU vote and every GATT negotiation.

One element of doubt about Nick Crafts's presentation lies in his account of the improvements in the skills of the British labour force. This appears to be contradicted by reports of OECD measures of literacy and numeracy to which he refers. According to these, British 16 to 25-year-olds performed less well in the mid-1990s than 26 to 35-year-olds, which indicates a ten-year fall in the quality of the education that British schools have been delivering. Worse still, the average literacy and numeracy standards that British 16 to 25-year-olds achieve rank fourteenth of the fifteen advanced countries tested. Crafts adds that agency problems are potentially severe in the provision of state schooling, where there is little direct connection between the education that schools provide and the standards of achievement that parents and pupils desire. Independent schools that have to market education are under continual competitive pressure, so they suffer no comparable agency hiatuses. There will be great improvement in welfare and the skills and health of the population if, over the next decades, the progress that Britain has undoubtedly achieved in the resolution of agency problems in industry and commerce, documented so fully by Nick Crafts, can be matched by similar advances in the provision of public health and education.

This Foreword opened with the great improvements in life expectation and in material living standards which Britain has achieved since 1870. It would be strange if, in reversal of this progress, education and health have actually been moving backwards over the last decade. If Britain is as well placed to exploit the

IT revolution as Nick Crafts supposes, a good deal of education will actually have been quite effectively directed. He is therefore surely right to emphasise Britain's positive achievements in education and training; but his presentation of the data is so detailed and balanced that it will often be possible for his readers to take a different view.

They will find far more in his rich and detailed presentation than I have been able to draw to their attention in this Foreword.

WALTER ELTIS
Oxford University
April 2002

As with all IEA publications, the views expressed in Professor Craft's paper are those of the author, not those of the Institute (which has no corporate view), its managing trustees, Academic Advisory Council or senior staff.

SUMMARY

- Since 1870 Britain has experienced a long period of relative economic decline, which was at its most pronounced from the 1950s through the 1970s and has not yet begun to be reversed.
- Nevertheless, average living standards improved more during the 20th century than would have been thought possible in earlier centuries – and more than the national accounts show, because of gains in life expectancy and reductions in working time. Claims that 'sustainable economic welfare' has declined recently should be regarded with scepticism.
- Relative economic decline has stemmed from weak productivity performance rather than from low investment; innovation capacity in Britain also seems relatively poor. However, the growth potential of the British economy is well above what it was a century ago
- Britain's productivity gap with the United States before World War II was due mainly to 'lack of technological congruence': postwar failure to catch up as rapidly as other European countries resulted primarily from 'social capability' problems. After 1945 Britain suffered from incentive structures which adversely affected investment, innovation and policy-making.
- Up to the late 1970s there was significant government failure (as well as market failure) in Britain. Governments failed to

strengthen competition; policies such as extensive nationalisation were badly designed; supply-side reforms – especially in industrial relations – were not undertaken; and governments succumbed to interest-group pressures to delay restructuring.

- The Thatcher governments took a new approach which included privatisation and deregulation, less emphasis on industrial policy, reform of industrial relations, restraints on government spending, tax restructuring, changes in vocational training, and expansion of higher education.

- In principle, if not always in practice, the new approach was consistent with the insights of modern growth economics, especially where agency problems prevailed.

- The productivity growth record of the 1990s is mixed: relative economic decline with regard to other European countries may have ceased but it has not clearly been reversed. However, the outcome is much better than might have been predicted in 1979.

- The reforms pursued by the Conservatives since 1979, and largely accepted by New Labour, have improved the incentive structures facing firms and workers. A programme of microeconomic reform, to improve productivity performance, is promised: it is important that government failure does not get in the way.

- The revolution in information and communications technology is central to long-run prospects. Substantial managerial effort is required to reap the benefits in terms of improved productivity. Early signs are encouraging, even though the UK was outpaced by the US late in the 20th century.

TABLES AND FIGURES

Britain's Relative Economic Performance, 1870–1999

1 INTRODUCTION[1]

This paper offers an overview of long-run economic perform-ance. Its main aim is to set out the details of British economic growth from the point where relative economic decline is com-monly believed to have begun to the present. Before attempting this it is important to establish a context, and this is the principal task of this Introduction. Several aspects need to be developed. They include setting out some key ideas from the theory of eco-nomic growth, distinguishing market failure and government fail-ure as alternative explanations of shortfalls in British productivity, delineating major breaks in supply-side policy, and reviewing key claims from the historiography of British decline. First of all, how-ever, some measurement issues are considered.

Measurement issues

Traditionally, economists have taken the long-run or trend rate of growth of real gross domestic product (GDP) per person to be the best available measure of an economy's achievement in raising liv-ing standards and the level of (purchasing power parity adjusted) real GDP per person to be the standard of economic performance

---

1 This paper has benefited substantially from joint work with Mary O'Mahony but I am responsible for all errors.

across countries at a point in time. This seems to be broadly consistent with the competitiveness agenda which focuses on success in production. An extension to this is to measure net national product (NNP), which takes account of net external income flows and deducts depreciation of capital from GDP to estimate the sustainable level of personal consumption or national income.

At the same time, economists have also recognised that there are strong reasons to consider augmenting real GDP or NNP as defined in the national income accounts to obtain a more comprehensive measure of real national income or economic welfare. Three additional considerations are particularly worth noting:

a) An economy with the same GDP but more leisure per person is better off. Given that both over time and across countries the amount of time spent in market work has varied greatly, it is desirable to take this into account in comparisons of living standards.

b) It is generally agreed that increases in life expectancy have made a substantial addition to consumer welfare during the twentieth century. There exists market-based evidence about willingness to pay for reduced hazards, so estimating a monetary value of improved longevity is possible.

c) It is also widely accepted that NNP is an inadequate measure of sustainable consumption. Environmentalists have stressed the importance of taking into account depletion of natural resources and pollution and have made a number of other criticisms of the national accounts concept of national income.

All these are important points and they are examined in what follows. It should be accepted, however, that there is no consensus on how best to incorporate these components of well-being into an expanded set of national accounts and that measurement (index number) problems loom larger than with the (less ambitious) approach based simply on real GDP.

Moreover, although economic growth is central to the enhancement of living standards, other outcomes may also matter a good deal. Indeed, ultimately, value judgements are required to weight these relative to economic growth. For example, it might be argued that most people are risk-averse and would give up some extra growth for a reduction of economic insecurity if that choice were available. If less inequality in income distribution were regarded as a good thing, an acceleration of trend growth where the rich gain more than the poor might be seen as an adverse development by those who value equality highly.

The notion of British relative economic decline is inherently based on international comparisons. Whether the criterion is real GDP per person or some broader measure of economic welfare there is no doubt that, in common with all the OECD countries, Britain's absolute living standards have improved over time. The disappointment for Britain has been that growth elsewhere has been faster and that, as a result, Britain has tended over time to slide down the league tables. This was notably the case during the 'Golden Age' of European economic growth in the years after World War II when British economic growth was at an all-time high yet the acceleration in growth elsewhere was much stronger.

A key reason for being interested in comparisons, whether over time or across countries, is to obtain a yardstick against which to assess what may have been possible. To be meaningful, however, it is vital to choose a suitable peer group and to normalise for differences in circumstances. Thus, it might be argued that the macroeconomic environment for growth during the Golden Age was exceptionally benign, and it is surely important to allow for the scope for follower countries to catch up with the leaders to create phases of very rapid productivity growth (as in Japan in the 1950s and 1960s). Comparisons should relate to long-run trend growth and should be aware that lack of synchronisation of cyclical fluctuations in economic activity can distort relative growth performance over short periods.

Key ideas from growth economics

There have been important developments recently in thinking about growth. A major theme in economic history has been the exploration of success and failure in catch-up growth, i.e. in the performance of countries seeking to reduce the productivity gap with the leading country, which throughout the twentieth century was the United States. The very influential approach of Abramovitz and David (1996) highlights the central roles of technological congruence and social capability. The former relates to the transferability of the leader's technology to the follower countries where its cost-effectiveness will depend on relative factor prices, the availability of skilled labour, market size, etc. It may be quite rational not to adopt the leader's technology elsewhere where cost or demand circumstances are different. Broadly speaking, American technology based on cheap energy inputs and mass production was not well suited to European conditions before World War II but was much more suitable in the later decades of the twentieth century.

Social capability refers to a society's effectiveness in assimilating technology both in terms of rapidity and realisation of its productivity potential. This depends both on how well markets function and on how successful governments are in creating incentive structures that promote economic efficiency. Success in catch-up growth requires institutions and policies that facilitate investment, innovation and technology transfer and prevent vested interests from obstructing the growth process.

The recognition that social capability matters for growth has a parallel in that growth theory has increasingly recognised the importance of microeconomic foundations. The chief insight that is relevant to the analysis is that growth outcomes are crucially dependent on incentive structures which are shaped by a wide range of microeconomic policies decided by politicians whose own incentives therefore also matter. Two key points deserve to be highlighted.

First, the driving force of long-run growth is technological progress (both through invention and technology transfer) which is brought about through 'endogenous innovation', that is by attempts to reduce costs and develop new products in the pursuit of profit. Well-designed policy and institutions can increase innovative activities by increasing expected returns for a given volume of effort. In this context, productive expenditure by government, say, on infrastructure or human capital will have a positive effect but distortionary taxation a negative effect on growth.

Second, the central role of innovation in economic growth highlights the importance of 'creative destruction' in which technologies become obsolete and firms exit. Thus, it has been estimated that in British manufacturing since 1980 about half of all total factor productivity (TFP) growth comes from the reallocation of production from losers to winners in this process (Disney *et al.*, 2000). In such cases job losses are good news for productivity performance but are rarely acclaimed as such by the press or by politicians. Slowing down or blocking exit of the inefficient is a perennial temptation for politicians, who can clearly identify the votes of the losers to be helped but cannot expect any reward for the promise that their pain will be good for the living standards of unidentified future citizens on average.

Market failure and government failure

The notion of market failure is familiar from elementary micro-economics. An efficient allocation of resources requires that marginal benefit is equal to marginal social cost. There are, of course, well-known cases where markets will fail to achieve this result; these include situations of market power in which output is restricted and price exceeds marginal cost, activities characterised by externalities such as pollution where marginal social cost exceeds marginal private cost, and the provision of public goods such as defence which are characterised by non-excludability.

Economic growth has traditionally been thought to be quite vulnerable to market failures, especially with regard to human capital formation, research and development (R & D) and the learning by doing associated with infant industries. In each case, it is argued that there are spillover effects that imply sub-optimal investment because investors cannot appropriate all the returns. This tendency for the social rate of return to exceed the private rate of return has frequently been adduced as a *prima facie* justification for government intervention, for example, in the form of subsidies to eliminate underinvestment and bring marginal private and social benefits into line.

A different type of market failure is where cost curves are

higher than they need be because of insufficient managerial effort to adopt profitable technologies and/or eliminate unnecessary expenditures, e.g. on overstaffing. Such outcomes are most likely to occur with imperfect information, where the owners of firms do not effectively monitor the actions of managers and cannot devise contracts that align the managers' interests with their own. Monitoring of management runs into potential free-rider problems unless there are shareholders with substantial holdings who can largely internalise the gains. Incentivising managers is easier in cases where there are observable yardsticks based on outperforming rivals. Thus, competitive pressure from the presence (or perhaps even the potential entry) of rival firms helps to eliminate productivity shortfalls of this kind, but this may be absent in cases where market power results from barriers to entry. With diffuse shareholding, a hostile takeover process can address managerial failure to innovate, but the takeover threat may undermine incentives to make long-term investments. This suggests that dominant shareholders, or in their absence competition, will promote productivity growth (Nickell, 1996).

Moreover, in designing policy to promote faster growth, it becomes important to distinguish between profit-maximising firms and so-called 'conservative' firms in which principal-agent problems loom large, i.e. when managers pursue their own objectives to the detriment of shareholders. There, managers who are not tightly controlled by shareholders delay cost-reducing initiatives which require effort to discover and implement, subject to the constraint of keeping the firm afloat.

Aghion *et al.* (1997) provide the following tableau of the impacts of these agency costs on the adoption of new technology (Figure 1).

Figure 1 **Policy impact on the rate of technology adoption**

	profit-maximising firm	conservative firm
competition policy	*negative*	positive
industrial policy	positive	*negative*

For profit-maximising firms, industrial policy in the form of subsidies to innovation speeds up adoption by raising profitability, but strong competition policy tends to reduce innovation by making it harder to appropriate returns. For conservative firms, industrial policy cushions managers and thus reduces innovative effort while competition policy does the opposite.

The traditional presumptions that market failures justify government intervention and can be expected to be remedied by effective government action are not necessarily valid, as the increasing attention paid to government failure in the academic literature has taught us (Wallis and Dollery, 1999). Government actions 'to improve the workings of markets' may be ineffective or even do more harm than good. This is not simply a rehearsal of the old 'equity versus efficiency' conflict where redistribution of income has a cost, which voters may accept, in distortionary taxation that inhibits capital accumulation. With regard to relative economic decline three aspects of government failure, which have already been foreshadowed in the analysis, are particularly relevant.

First, policies address market failures but are badly designed or misconceived. For example, the effect of subsidies which only give a weak stimulus to productivity performance may be outweighed by the impact of the distortionary taxation used to finance them, or a failure to recognise the importance of agency problems within firms might result in an inappropriate balance between industrial and competition policy.

Second, interventions aimed at correcting market failures are vitiated by agency problems within the public sector. For example, nationalisation might be intended to deal with abuse of market power or under-provision of public goods but lead to low productivity/high cost outcomes because of inadequate monitoring and/or incentivising of managers. Similarly, international comparisons suggest that the attainments of schoolchildren are not closely correlated with public expenditure on education but do depend strongly on effectiveness in dealing with principal-agent problems in the delivery of effective teaching (Wössmann, 2000).

Third, a central aspect of the incentive structures facing politicians is that votes may often be lost by pursuing policies that promote economic efficiency and higher productivity. A classic example is the attraction of protectionism to vote-seeking governments despite its generally adverse impact on productivity growth and overall economic welfare. Such policies heavily reward relatively small but well-organised and easily identified groups of producers at the expense of small losses per person for a large but disparate group of consumers for whom it is not worth incurring the costs of mounting a protest. Exactly the same political calculus applies to allowing the process of creative destruction to flourish.

A brief history of supply-side policy

There have been massive swings in supply-side policy since the late nineteenth century, and the aim here is simply to convey the flavour of different epochs while more detailed treatment is left to later chapters. In this spirit, Table 1 reports basic and top rates of income tax in snapshot years as a symptom of the stance taken in different eras.

Table 1 **UK income tax rates (per cent): selected years, 1870–2001**

	Basic rate	Top rate
1870	2.1	2.1
1914	5.8	13.3
1938	25.0	62.5
1949	45.0	97.5
1973	38.75	88.75
2001	22.0	40.0

Source: Mitchell (1988).

Prior to World War I there was little in the way of active state intervention and taxation remained at a low level even after the welfare reforms introduced by the 1906 Liberal government, with revenues in 1913 still only 10.7 per cent of GDP (Middleton, 1996). Britain participated fully in the globalisation of the period, maintaining free trade and free movement of capital. There was neither competition policy nor industrial policy. The main policy initiative likely to have enhanced productivity was a vigorous expansion of education, although enrolments in secondary schools were still very low in 1913 at 5.5 per cent of the age group. Nevertheless, major developments in the period from 1890 onward saw the spread of polytechnics, technical colleges and universities, together with the introduction of free and compulsory elementary education (Sanderson, 1999).

In the inter-war period, supply-side policy was largely driven by the exigencies of coping with external shocks from a disintegrating world economy traumatised by depression and retreating into deglobalisation. The state began to play a larger role in terms of industrial policy, which attempted rationalisation of declining staple industries such as coal and cotton, although not competition policy. Indeed, by the 1930s free trade had been superseded by a general tariff and encouragement of cartels was the order of the day. By 1937 tax revenues had reached 21.6 per cent of GDP. Educational expansion continued but rather lost its impetus, and still only 9.9 per cent of the 13–18 age group were in secondary education in 1937. An interesting development was state expenditure on R & D, although this was primarily for military purposes and comprised only about 0.1 per cent of GDP (Edgerton, 1996).

From World War II to the 1970s the move to state intervention went much farther, prompted by a widespread loss of faith in the market economy. Tax revenues moved ahead to 30 to 35 per cent of GDP, the energy and transport sectors became nationalised industries, and industrial policy became much more ambitious, notably through subsidising private-sector investment and supporting national champions. By the mid-1970s public-sector investment and subsidies to producers had risen to 10.8 per cent and 7.6 per cent of GDP respectively, compared with 3.6 per cent and 0.7 per cent respectively in 1938 (Middleton, 1996). Substantial expansion of educational provision resumed, and by the mid-1970s public expenditure on education had risen to 5.9 per cent of GDP compared with 2.1 per cent in 1938, while secondary school enrolment had risen to 73 per cent. State support of R & D also expanded markedly (although, as before World War II, about two-thirds was for military purposes), to reach 1.4 per cent of GDP in the 1960s (Edgerton, 1996). Competition policy initiatives also emerged with the establishment of the Monopolies and Restrictive Practices Commission in 1948, followed by tough anti-cartel legislation in 1956 and weak restrictions on mergers from 1965, while tariffs were reduced under the auspices of the GATT and Britain participated in the gradual resumption of globalisation.

The election of the Thatcher government in 1979 saw a marked change in direction in supply-side policy, which in most important respects has been sustained by Labour since 1997. Broadly speaking, this has involved a shift away from industrial towards competition policy. This has entailed the privatisation of most state enterprises, including the sectors nationalised after the war, a substantial reduction of state aids to industry, and a strengthening of competitive pressures on enterprises mainly through deregulation and signing up to the Single Market under the Conservatives and by a beefing up of competition policy under Labour. Regional selective assistance, which had been £1.87 billion in 1990 prices in 1975/76, fell to £0.2 billion in the late 1990s (Taylor and Wren, 1997), while public-sector net investment, which had been 5.8 per cent of GDP in 1975, fell to 0.4 per cent by 1998.

This should not, of course, be construed as a return to a pre-war, still less a Victorian, policy stance. Tax revenues stabilised at around 35 per cent of GDP. Educational enrolment for teenagers rose steeply in this period so that 69.5 per cent of the fifteen-to-nineteen age group were in full-time education by 1998. Government expenditure on R & D fell markedly to 0.6 per cent of GDP by 1997, but this decrease from earlier levels was entirely accounted for by a withdrawal from military R & D (Stoneman, 1999).

Historiography

One of the most celebrated arguments in British economic history relates to alleged 'entrepreneurial failure' in the late Victorian and Edwardian economies, culminating in the overtaking of Britain by its rivals. The most famous proponent of this view has been Landes (1969), who stressed technological and scientific incompetence and failure to embrace the second industrial revolution of cars, electricity and organic chemicals, and recently reasserted his position in unreconstructed fashion: 'one is inclined to define the British disease as a case of hard tardiness; entrepreneurial constipation' (1998: 455).

On reflection, this is clearly an allegation of market failure, since in a well-functioning market economy such poor performance would be eliminated through entry and exit and profitable opportunities in new ventures would be eagerly embraced. This has been made explicit in other versions of the argument, notably, for example, by Kennedy (1987) in his indictment of Victorian capital markets for failings that inhibited the finance of innovation and led to the systematic neglect of technologically promising investment opportunities, and by Elbaum and Lazonick (1986). These authors argued that the British experience 'runs directly counter to the neoclassical presumption that atomistic market competition is the best guarantor of economic well-being' and that 'entrenched institutional structures – in industrial relations, enterprise and market organization, education, finance, international trade and state-enterprise relations – constrained the transformation of Britain's productive system' (1986: 2).

Not surprisingly, writers of this school of thought argue that relative decline prior to World War I, or indeed World War II, could have been averted by government intervention. For example, Aldcroft and Richardson claimed that infant industry tariffs would have been desirable to prevent 'over-commitment' to the old staple industries but that 'only a planned economy could have pushed forward the development of the new industries to the required level before 1914' (1969: 195). Elbaum and Lazonick again: 'what British industry in general required was the visible hand of co-ordinated control, not the invisible hand of the self-regulating market' . . . 'state policy is implicated in British decline by virtue of its failure to intervene in the economy more decisively' (1986: 10–11).

The rebuttal of Landes's views by neoclassical economic historians was immediate and vigorous. In a very well-known paper, McCloskey concluded that the pre-1914 British economy was 'growing as rapidly as permitted by the growth of its resources and the effective exploitation of the available technology' (1970: 451). This claim had its underpinnings in McCloskey's strong belief that markets worked efficiently both in the allocation of capital and in applying competitive pressure that eliminated inefficient management of enterprises. The sub-text of this view was made more explicit by Broadberry: 'it seems unlikely that Britain could have avoided falling behind [the United States] during this period on account of her inferior resource endowments' (1997: 2).

Middleton (1996) pointed out that the critics of government inactivity had been far from specific in setting out what government should have done. He noted that the beginnings of state intervention in the inter-war period were inauspicious and hardly a good advertisement for a more activist policy stance prior to World War I: 'Government did little to improve the underlying position either directly or indirectly. It failed to change the market order to lessen the institutional rigidities and, if anything, established behaviours and expectations which were to the long run detriment of the British economy' (1996: 412–13).

Two basic positions are clearly discernible in this controversy over the pre-1914 British economy. The first is that markets failed to achieve either a much-needed restructuring of the economy or the efficient management of business enterprises while government did nothing about this. The second is that there was no significant failure of the market economy and the overtaking of Britain by the United States was unavoidable. No one, however, is alleging government failure in the sense of ill-judged or vote-seeking interventions that seriously damaged growth prospects. The literature on the equally contentious evaluation of the post-1945 British economy offers quite a contrast.

It is generally agreed that there was an avoidable aspect to the relative economic decline associated with both government and market failures in the postwar period, although the magnitude of this is disputed, as is the claim that it was effectively dealt with after 1979 (Middleton, 2000). Opinions are divided, however, as to what were the key market failures and whether this implies that government policy was misdirected or merely rather inept. A common theme, however, echoing Landes, has been continuing criticism of inferior British business organisation and management that resulted in low levels of investment and low rates of innovation (Alford, 1996).

On the left it is still maintained that capital market failures have required public direction of investment, that state-led industrial change was badly needed in postwar Britain but opportunities to carry this out effectively were wasted, notably by the Labour governments of the 1960s and 1970s, and that the shift to 'market-led liberalism' of the 1980s was both a massive error and a return to an approach that had failed Britain in the inter-war period (Coates, 1994). On the right it is argued that growth of the public sector during the 1960s and 1970s destabilised the economy by crowding out private investment and undermined economic growth, and that Thatcherism brought an end to these damaging developments (Bacon and Eltis, 1996).

A more mainstream school of thought points to the enhanced importance of R & D and education in postwar economic growth, and regrets continuing failures in the design of government policies to correct market failures in this area. For example, Sanderson (1999) drew attention to the persistent deficiencies in the training of non-academic teenagers that have held back economic growth through contributing to serious skill shortages, and Stoneman (1999) questioned the desirability of launch aid for civil aerospace projects. Writers in this tradition have also been disappointed by the apparent failure of industrial policy to promote growth in the interventionist period (Morris and Stout, 1985) and by the ineptitude with which a good deal of the privatisation programme of the 1980s and 1990s was implemented (Bishop *et al.*, 1994).

Owen (1999) went farther than this. He not only agreed that industrial policy retarded modernisation of the economy in the 1960s and 1970s, he also argued that the other major policy oversight of the postwar period has been the failure to strengthen competition enough: 'There is no doubt that some British companies were badly managed in the 1950s and 1960s and that there was a significant improvement in the 1980s and 1990s ... an important factor was the increasing intensity of competition ... To the extent that there were management weaknesses in Britain after the Second World War, they stemmed ... from soft markets' (1999: 422–3). Thus, his diagnosis takes common cause with that of economists like Nickell (1996) who have stressed the need for competition to combat agency problems in British firms.

Thus, a central issue emerges from this historiographic review. To what extent is relative economic decline to be attributed to government failure rather than market failure? Before any assessment can be made it is important to examine the historical record of

British economic growth in comparison with that of its peer group. This will be the agenda of Chapters 2 and 3, before we return to competing interpretations of relative economic decline in Chapters 4 and 5.

2 RELATIVE ECONOMIC DECLINE: AN INITIAL OVERVIEW

This chapter provides a basic statistical outline of comparative economic performance since 1870. The estimates are almost entirely based on data taken from well-known authoritative sources. Obviously, there are imperfections in all historical statistics and, in general, these are more serious the farther back one goes. The basic data used for the core description of Tables 2 to 5 are the best currently on offer, but they may eventually be revised if new information becomes available.

Table 2 gives a series of snapshots of relative levels of real GDP per person in benchmark years from 1870 to 1999. The estimates are based on historical national accounts data. The countries selected for comparison are determined partly by data availability and partly by including the OECD countries and recent Asian success stories with which Britain is regularly compared in everyday discussion. How far this is an appropriate peer group will be explored later. Former communist countries are excluded, although the source from which these numbers were taken does include provisional estimates. The table is not a complete list of all countries with high income in each year; for example, in 1913 Argentina's real GDP per person was $3,797 and, in 1950, Venezuela's was $7,462 (Maddison, 2001: 195).

The unit of measurement in Table 2 is 'International Dollars of 1990'. This means that current price estimates of GDP in the

Table 2 Levels of real GDP/person: benchmark years, 1870–1999 ($ 1990 international)

	1870		1913		1950		1973		1999	
1	Australia	3,645	Australia	5,715	USA	9,561	Switzerland	18,204	USA	27,975
2	UK	3,191	USA	5,301	Switzerland	9,064	USA	16,689	Norway	23,717
3	Netherlands	2,753	New Zealand	5,152	New Zealand	8,453	Canada	13,838	Singapore	23,582
4	New Zealand	2,704	UK	4,921	Australia	7,493	Denmark	13,945	Denmark	22,389
5	Belgium	2,697	Canada	4,447	Canada	7,437	Sweden	13,493	Switzerland	21,609
6	USA	2,445	Switzerland	4,266	Denmark	6,946	Germany	13,152	Canada	21,331
7	Switzerland	2,202	Belgium	4,220	UK	6,907	France	13,123	Australia	21,045
8	Denmark	2,003	Netherlands	4,049	Netherlands	6,738	Netherlands	13,082	Netherlands	20,805
9	Germany	1,913	Denmark	3,912	Sweden	5,996	Australia	12,759	Japan	20,431
10	France	1,876	Germany	3,833	Norway	5,463	New Zealand	12,513	Germany	20,415
11	Austria	1,863	France	3,485	Belgium	5,462	Belgium	12,170	Hong Kong	20,352
12	Ireland	1,775	Austria	3,465	France	5,270	UK	12,022	France	20,054
13	Canada	1,695	Sweden	3,096	Germany	4,281	Japan	11,439	Belgium	19,892
14	Sweden	1,664	Ireland	2,736	Finland	4,253	Norway	11,246	Ireland	19,756
15	Italy	1,499	Italy	2,564	Austria	3,706	Austria	11,235	Sweden	19,380
16	Norway	1,432	Norway	2,501	Italy	3,502	Finland	11,085	Austria	19,264
17	Spain	1,376	Spain	2,255	Ireland	3,446	Italy	10,643	UK	19,030
18	Finland	1,140	Finland	2,111	Spain	2,397	Spain	8,739	Finland	19,012
19	Portugal	997	Greece	1,592	Singapore	2,219	Greece	7,655	Italy	17,994
20	Greece	913	Japan	1,385	Hong Kong	2,218	Portugal	7,343	Taiwan	15,720
21	Japan	737	Singapore	1,279	Portugal	2,069	Hong Kong	7,104	New Zealand	15,355
22			Portugal	1,244	Japan	1,926	Ireland	6,867	Spain	14,746
23			South Korea	893	Greece	1,915	Singapore	5,977	South Korea	13,317
24			Taiwan	747	Taiwan	936	Taiwan	4,117	Portugal	13,289
25					South Korea	770	South Korea	2,841	Greece	11,620

Sources: Derived from Maddison (2001), updated to 1999 using World Bank (2001). Estimates for Germany refer to the area of West Germany prior to unification throughout from Maddison (1995); 1999 figure extrapolated from 1994 using growth rate of unified Germany.

currencies in each country in 1990 have been converted into dollars using a measure of the purchasing power of the currency rather than at the prevailing exchange rate. This is now standard practice in making international comparisons to avoid distortions arising from exchange rate volatility and systematic biases from divergences in prices of output in non-traded sectors. It must be remembered, however, that comparisons of purchasing power involve comparing the costs of baskets of goods and services and are subject to all the usual 'index number problems' to do with choices of weights, comparison of quality, etc. The basis of Table 2 is the database in Maddison (2001), which is the most widely used, but readers seeking an alternative can turn to Prados de la Escocura (1999).

Having obtained a measure of relative GDP per person for the base year, this is projected backward to 1870 and forward to 1999 using domestic estimates for the growth of real GDP in each country to obtain estimates of output per person in constant prices. Here too there are familiar index number problems in devising the appropriate price indices with which to deflate current price estimates of nominal GDP. Three particularly difficult issues concern the treatment of new goods, the measurement of quality changes over time and the value of output in non-marketed services. Nevertheless, the broad outline of relative performance shown in Table 2 is probably reasonably reliable for our purposes.

In assembling the figures from which Table 2 is taken, Maddison (2001) attempted to construct figures for these countries as currently constituted. For the UK, for example, the estimates exclude southern Ireland prior to 1921. Clearly, Germany is the most problematic case in this context. The estimates for Germany in Table 2 relate to the area of West Germany prior to unification.

Table 2 reflects the triumph of the United States in the first half of the twentieth century and the remarkable rise of East Asian countries in the second half of the century. Rapid advance in Europe between 1950 and 1973 is a feature of the table, which also reflects a steady decline in real GDP per person in the UK relative to other countries against a background of large increases in absolute levels brought about by economic growth.

Thus real GDP per person in 1999 was almost six times the 1870 level, yet the UK had slipped from second in 1870 to seventeenth by 1999. Prior to 1950, with the exception of Denmark and Switzerland, the UK was only overtaken by non-European countries. By the end of the 1970s, a further seven western European countries overtook the UK. During the period of economic reform since 1979 under the Conservatives and New Labour, the UK has not regained its lead over any of these countries, and has been overtaken by Ireland and three Asian countries, namely Hong Kong, Japan and Singapore.

Table 3 considers the period since 1870 in terms of growth rates rather than levels of real GDP per person. The periodisation is that of Maddison (2001), who analyses historical experience in terms of phases of economic growth. These are punctuated by wars, with 1913–50 comprising an episode both of war and of the dislocation of the inter-war depression. The 1950–73 period is one of generally very rapid growth followed by slowdown since the early 1970s, accompanied by a renewal of macroeconomic shocks and the evaporation of rapid catch-up growth in Europe and Japan.

The UK shares in this general experience, with 1950–73 showing the highest sustained growth rate in our economic history, but in every period it has had a below-average growth rate. In

Table 3 **Rates of growth of real GDP/person: selected periods, 1870–1999 (per cent per year)**

1870–1913		1913–50		1950–73		1973–99	
Australia	1.0	Australia	0.7	USA	2.4	Switzerland	0.7
UK	1.0	USA	1.6	Switzerland	3.1	USA	2.0
Netherlands	0.9	New Zealand	1.4	New Zealand	1.7	Canada	1.7
New Zealand	1.5	UK	0.9	Australia	2.3	Denmark	1.8
Belgium	1.0	Canada	1.4	Canada	2.7	Sweden	1.4
USA	1.8	Switzerland	2.1	Denmark	3.1	Germany	1.7
Switzerland	1.6	Belgium	0.7	UK	2.4	France	1.7
Denmark	1.6	Netherlands	1.1	Sweden	3.1	Netherlands	1.8
Germany	1.6	Denmark	1.6	Netherlands	3.4	Australia	1.9
France	1.4	Germany	0.3	Norway	3.2	New Zealand	0.8
Austria	1.4	France	1.1	Belgium	3.6	Belgium	1.9
Ireland	1.0	Austria	0.2	France	4.0	UK	1.8
Canada	2.3	Sweden	2.1	Germany	5.0	Japan	2.3
Sweden	1.5	Ireland	0.7	Finland	4.2	Norway	2.9
Italy	1.3	Italy	0.8	Austria	4.9	Austria	2.1
Norway	1.3	Norway	2.1	Italy	5.0	Finland	2.1
Spain	1.2	Spain	0.2	Ireland	3.0	Italy	2.0
Finland	1.4	Finland	1.9	Spain	5.8	Spain	2.0
Portugal	0.5	Greece	0.5	Singapore	4.4	Greece	1.6
Greece	1.3	Japan	0.9	Hong Kong	5.2	Portugal	2.3
Japan	1.5	Singapore	1.5	Portugal	5.7	Hong Kong	4.1
		Portugal	1.4	Japan	8.0	Ireland	4.1
		South Korea	(0.4)	Greece	6.2	Singapore	5.4
		Taiwan	0.6	Taiwan	6.6	Taiwan	5.3
				South Korea	5.8	South Korea	6.1

Source: Derived from Table 2.

1870–1913, the UK ranks 15th out of 21, in 1913–50 13th of 24, in 1950–73 22nd of 25, and in 1973–99 15th of 25. In the postwar years, it is noticeable that the gap between the British growth rate and that of the fastest-growing economies has been much larger than before. In the most recent period since 1973 the growth rate of 1.8 per cent is lower than during the Golden Age but above that of the pre-World War II periods. The gap between the British and the median growth rate has narrowed during the post-Golden Age slowdown from 1.6 percentage points to 0.2 percentage points.

In Table 3, the countries are listed in the rank order of their real GDP per person at the start of each period. Since World War II, but not before, there is a tendency – pronounced in 1950–73 – for growth rates to be inversely related to initial income levels as might be predicted if catch-up was a strong part of growth performance. In this regard, it is noticeable that British growth appears to have been unimpressive relative to countries with a similar starting point both before and after 1973.

In the Introduction it was noted that, in considering relative levels of economic welfare, it is important to look at how much work effort is needed to produce GDP. This is, in fact, much more important both in international and in intertemporal comparisons than is generally realised. Hours worked have changed enormously over time but experience has diverged, especially with regard to Europe versus Asia. For example, the estimates in Crafts (1997, 1999) show annual hours worked per person employed in the UK falling from 2,984 in 1870 to 2,224 in 1950 and 1,732 in 1996, whereas in South Korea an average work year of 2,200 hours in 1950 rose to 2,453 by 1996.

Table 4 reports estimates of real GDP per hour worked and provides some interesting modifications to the picture given in Table 2. The overall growth rate of British hourly labour productivity in the long run is higher than that of real GDP per person; the level of 1996 was 8.9 times higher than that of 1870. Relative economic decline on this measure is similar, however, as the UK falls from second in 1870 to sixteenth in 1996. Nevertheless, in 1996 the UK remains above all the East Asian countries, including Hong Kong, Japan and Singapore, in terms of hourly labour productivity.

Table 4 Levels of real GDP/hours worked: benchmark years, 1870–1996 ($ 1990 international)

	1870		1913		1950		1973		1996	
1	Australia	3.18	Australia	5.48	USA	13.47	USA	23.40	Norway	32.82
2	UK	2.55	USA	5.09	Canada	10.32	Netherlands	18.89	Netherlands	32.04
3	Netherlands	2.43	Canada	4.44	Australia	9.01	Canada	18.54	Belgium	30.50
4	USA	2.24	UK	4.30	Switzerland	8.87	Switzerland	18.54	France	29.94
5	Belgium	2.17	Netherlands	4.11	Netherlands	7.18	Sweden	18.02	Germany	29.26
6	Switzerland	1.77	Belgium	3.68	Sweden	7.08	Australia	17.24	USA	27.44
7	Canada	1.68	Denmark	3.53	UK	6.91	Belgium	16.90	Italy	26.82
8	Germany	1.58	Germany	3.50	Belgium	6.19	Germany	16.58	Denmark	25.83
9	Denmark	1.57	Switzerland	3.30	Denmark	6.08	Denmark	16.57	Sweden	25.35
10	Austria	1.38	Austria	2.91	Norway	5.47	France	16.16	Ireland	24.87
11	France	1.37	France	2.88	France	5.46	Austria	15.17	Australia	24.79
12	Sweden	1.22	Sweden	2.58	Germany	4.98	Norway	14.21	Austria	24.60
13	Norway	1.10	Norway	2.21	Finland	4.12	UK	13.93	Canada	24.41
14	Italy	1.05	Italy	2.14	Italy	4.05	Italy	13.62	Spain	23.50
15	Finland	0.86	Finland	1.86	Austria	4.04	Finland	12.31	Switzerland	23.49
16	Japan	0.46	Japan	1.07	Ireland	3.28	Spain	10.69	UK	22.68
17					Japan	2.83	Greece	10.60	Finland	22.31
18					Singapore	2.66	Japan	10.35	Japan	20.41
19					Greece	2.53	Portugal	9.57	Hong Kong	18.87
20					Portugal	2.50	Ireland	9.00	Singapore	17.53
21					Spain	2.38	Singapore	6.87	Greecee	16.81
22					Hong Kong	1.62	Hong Kong	6.73	Taiwan	16.02
23					South Korea	1.28	Taiwan	4.43	Portugal	13.67
24					Taiwan	1.04	South Korea	3.56	South Korea	11.70

Sources: Derived from Crafts (1997, 1999), updated using Maddison (2001) except for post-1950 France, Germany, Japan and USA, which rely on O'Mahony (1999).

Indeed, it is quite noticeable that, relative either to Asia or the USA, Europe looks much better in terms of output per hour worked than output per person. This reflects differences in age structures of the populations, retirement and holiday practices, and, of course, unemployment. This might be borne in mind by those who compile 'competitiveness' league tables, although the implications for socio-economic welfare are not entirely straightforward and deserve some research.

Table 5 disaggregates comparative productivity experience in terms of three broad sectors of activity whose relative importance has changed over time in all advanced economies as industrialisation has been followed by deindustrialisation. As Table 5 shows, although there are broad similarities in this experience across the OECD, the UK is highly unusual in terms of its very low share of agricultural employment in the nineteenth century. In all cases, however, the service sector is now hugely more important than it was in 1870.

This is important in understanding how Britain has been overtaken by Germany and the United States since 1870, as has been explored in depth by Broadberry (1998) and is apparent from Table 5. In 1870, the UK had a substantial labour productivity lead in services, but the USA had pulled well ahead by 1950 and Germany overtook the UK during the Golden Age. In 1990, in both cases, the service-sector labour productivity gap was about 30 per cent and accounted for most of the overall productivity gap. In industry (which includes construction, mining and utilities as well as manufacturing), a sizeable productivity gap with the USA was already evident in the mid-nineteenth century, and it rose dramatically in the Fordist era, but by 1990 was back to a level similar to that of 1870. A productivity gap in industry with Germany similar to that of 1990

Table 5 **Structural change and relative decline**

	— Employment shares (%) —			— Relative Output/Worker — (UK = 100)	
	UK	Germany	USA	Germany/UK	US/UK
1870					
Agriculture	22.2	49.5	50.0	55.7	86.9
Industry	42.4	29.1	24.8	86.2	153.6
Services	35.4	21.4	25.2	66.1	85.8
1910					
Agriculture	11.8	34.5	32.0	67.3	103.2
Industry	44.1	37.9	31.8	122.0	193.5
Services	44.1	27.6	36.2	81.3	107.3
1950					
Agriculture	5.1	24.3	11.0	41.2	126.0
Industry	46.5	42.1	32.9	95.8	243.9
Services	48.4	33.6	56.1	83.1	140.8
1973					
Agriculture	2.9	7.2	3.7	50.8	131.2
Industry	41.8	47.3	28.9	128.9	215.1
Services	55.3	45.5	67.4	111.0	137.3
1990					
Agriculture	2.0	3.4	2.5	75.4	151.1
Industry	28.5	39.7	21.8	116.7	163.0
Services	69.5	56.9	75.7	130.3	129.6

Source: Broadberry (2002).

had already opened up by 1910 when, in terms of GDP, Germany's relative standing was still held back by its large agricultural sector.

Tables 2 to 5 have considered economic performance as it has been traditionally measured through the national accounts. Table 6 reports estimates of the shadow (or hidden) economy and begins the second part of this chapter, which looks at extensions to and some criticisms of this conventional approach. There is general agreement that the share of economic activity that avoids measurement in the national accounts has been rising, probably

Table 6 'Shadow economies' as percentages of GDP

	1960	1970	1980	1998
Australia				14.1
Austria	0.4	1.8	3.0	9.1
Belgium		10.4	16.4	22.6
Canada			10.6	15.0
Denmark	4.3	6.4	8.6	18.4
France		3.9	6.9	14.9
Germany	2.0	2.8	10.8	14.7
Greece				29.0
Hong Kong				13.0
Ireland		4.3	8.0	16.3
Italy		10.7	16.7	27.8
Japan				11.3
Netherlands		4.8	9.1	13.5
Norway	1.5	6.5	10.6	19.7
Singapore				13.0
South Korea				38.0
Spain		10.3	17.2	23.4
Sweden	1.6	7.3	12.2	20.0
Switzerland	1.2	4.1	6.5	8.0
Taiwan				16.5
UK		2.0	8.4	13.0
USA	3.1	3.6	5.0	8.9

Sources: Schneider (2000); for Hong Kong, Singapore, South Korea and Taiwan (estimates for 1990) and Japan (estimate for 1997), Schneider and Enste (2000). In some cases estimates are mid-point of a range.

considerably, in OECD countries as the burden of tax and regulation has risen in recent decades (Schneider and Enste, 2000). Various methods have been proposed to estimate its size, all of which are somewhat problematic. The most widely used approach is based on inferences from the use of cash, and Table 6 mainly relies on this 'currency demand' methodology. If the estimate for the UK is accurate, it would imply that growth since 1973 has been understated by about 0.4 percentage points by the national accounts. Applying the correction factors suggested by Table 6 would not, however, make much difference to the rank order positions shown in Tables 2 and 4.

The UK shared in the remarkable improvement in life expectancy that the world experienced during the twentieth century, as Table 7 reports. This came largely from better public health and medical science and technology. There is ample evidence that individuals trade off risks to life and health for higher wages (Viscusi, 1993) and, in principle, it is reasonable therefore to ask how much extra consumption would be required to compensate the population for giving up their high life expectancy and leave them equally well off. In fact, this is similar to the willingness-to-pay approach used in social cost-benefit analysis of transport projects by the DETR when they use a value of a statistical life to estimate the benefits of reductions in fatal accident hazards. A specific version of this methodology has recently been developed by Nordhaus (1998) and has been adapted for use in Table 7. For details, see the Appendix below.

There is a strong claim in Table 7, namely that taking account of welfare gains from better life expectancy is potentially a very important addition to growth as measured by the national accounts. The calculated gains from this component in 1870–1913 and 1913–50 far outweigh growth in conventional GDP per person (by 2.0 to 1.0 and 2.0 to 0.8 per cent per year, respectively) and would double the growth rate in the recent past. Only in the Golden Age are they overshadowed by GDP growth. Obviously, the precise detail of the table cannot carry much weight because estimates of the value of a statistical life exist only for the recent past and are subject to quite wide margins of error, but the basic message does deserve to be taken seriously.

Table 7 **Imputation to real GDP growth for improved life expectancy (per cent per year)**

Life expectancy at birth		Imputation to growth	
1870	41.3	1870–1913	2.0
1913	53.4	1913–50	2.0
1950	69.2	1950–73	0.8
1973	72.0	1973–98	1.7
1998	77.1		

Source: Crafts (2001); imputation to growth based on method proposed by Nordhaus (1998) – see text.

The calculations in Table 7 provide a powerful reason for supposing that the national accounts tend to underestimate improvements in the standard of living, at least during the twentieth century. Many of those interested in issues of sustainability have tended to paint a much more pessimistic picture, and a widely quoted recent estimate has claimed that for the past quarter-century or so sustainable economic welfare has been in *absolute* decline in the UK (Jackson *et al.*, 1997). Clearly, this has not been reflected in real NNP as estimated by the national accounts but, as was noted in the Introduction, that concept may be inadequate as a measure of economic welfare.

The corrections that need to be made to NNP in this regard are well reviewed in Usher (1980) and Nordhaus (2000). They include deducting items that are really intermediate rather than final goods, such as the costs of commuting and defence spending, taking account both of the depletion of natural resources and additions to the stock of technological knowledge as well as depreciation of physical capital, and placing a value on changes in the availability of 'environmental goods' such as better health and greater leisure. This last concept, as defined by Usher (1980, ch. 7), comprises background conditions that are not included in the common understanding of income but changes in which would have a monetary-equivalent value to consumers.

Although revisions to the national accounts of this kind to obtain better measures of economic welfare would perhaps command quite widespread support in principle, there is no consensus about exactly how to proceed, and there are a number of very difficult technical issues to resolve. In the Appendix to Chapter 2, Table 9 and the accompanying description offer an illustration of how some of these adjustments might be implemented. The estimates presented there are rough and incomplete but they offer a strong message to the effect that the notion of absolute decline in the recent past should be taken with a huge pinch of salt.

The contrast in growth rates reported in Table 8 is dramatic. While the index of sustainable economic welfare (ISEW) shows considerable absolute decline in 1973–98 and suggests that the national accounts are totally misleading as a guide to sustainable income, the revised ISEW developed in Table 9 indicates that sustainable living standards have probably grown considerably faster than real GDP per person. Why is there such a difference?

The main reasons are as follows. First, ISEW gives no weight to welfare gains from longer life expectancy. Second, for the 1973–98 period ISEW contains a large negative adjustment to consumption for rising inequality; this is completely misplaced – it confuses a dislike for growth which actually favours the rich with the potential to sustain consumption for all. Third, ISEW sets aside too large a share of GDP for investment to maintain capital per person in the face of population growth because it takes no account of technological progress.

The overall picture that has emerged from this survey is easy to

Table 8 **Growth rates of different concepts of income/head compared (per cent per year)**

	Real GDP	Sustainable welfare	Revised ISEW*
1950–73	2.4	1.9	3.3
1973–98	1.8	-0.6	2.9

Sources: Col. 1: from sources for Table 2; col. 2: from Jackson *et al.* (1997), second period ends in 1996; col. 3: author's calculations based on Table 9.
*ISEW = Index of Sustainable Economic Welfare – see text.

summarise. Since 1870 there has been a long period of relative economic decline which was at its most pronounced in the years from the 1950s through the 1970s and has not yet started to be reversed. On the other hand, average living standards improved throughout the twentieth century by more than the national accounts reveal, and indeed by far more than could have been thought possible in earlier centuries. The claim that sustainable economic welfare has declined since the 1970s should be treated with extreme scepticism.

Appendix

This Appendix provides brief details of the calculations that underlie Tables 7 and 8. A fuller explanation can be found in Crafts (2002). Here I accept the approach in Jackson *et al.* (1997), where the amendments to the national accounts that they suggest are justified in principle, and retain these components of ISEW even though the empirical implementation may be controversial. This is not intended to be an endorsement of those particular estimates; the present concern is to examine how ISEW would change if it were adjusted to match the concept of utility-based national income (Nordhaus, 2000) more closely. The adjustments to the original ISEW made here are to incorporate gains from lower mortality, to remove the adjustment for rising inequality of income, and to take account of improvements in technology in evaluating the amount of investment necessary to sustain per capita consumption.

Table 7 uses the 'mortality approach' in Nordhaus (1998), which calculates the value of improved health status in a period of time by taking the change in age-specific mortality rates weighted by the age structure of the population times the estimated value of lower mortality derived from market-based estimates of the valuation of lower risks. This is shown to be a computationally convenient approximation to a 'life-years approach' in which the economic valuation of improved health equals the weighted average increase in life expectancy multiplied by the value of an additional year of life.

To implement this for the UK, Table 7 takes the base value of a statistical life in each year to be 132 times GDP per person based on the research reviewed in Miller (2000). The value of a statistical life is then age-weighted on the basis proposed by Murray (1996), where improvements in life expectancy are regarded as less valuable at very young and very old ages compared with the prime of life. This implies a base value for the last period (1973–98) at its mid-point in 1986 of £1.35 million at 1995 prices and £0.88 million after age-weighting is applied, while the fall in weighted mortality rates during the period was 4,988/million. This gives an estimate of the gain from lower mortality of $0.004988 \times 0.88 = 4,377$ or 42.7 per cent of 1986 GDP per person, which would add about 1.7 per cent to the growth rate. The other estimates in Table 7 are obtained in similar fashion.

Table 9 **Components of UK sustainable economic welfare/person, 1950, 1973 and 1998 (£ 1995)**

	1950	1973	1998
Positives			
Personal Consumption	2,960	4,904	8,246
Net Capital	105	612	1,259
Household Labour Services	1,153	1,788	2,755
Higher Life Expectancy	n/a	1,606	5,587
Negatives			
Consumption Revisions	368	790	2,054
Pollution and Environmental Damage	1,022	1,825	2,908
Natural Capital Depreciation	445	1,194	2,447
Revised ISEW	**2,383**	**5,101**	**10,438**

Sources: Crafts (2002); derived from Jackson *et al.* (1997) – adjustments described in the text.

The revised index of sustainable economic welfare in Table 9 was obtained as follows. The starting point is personal consumption from the national income accounts. To this is added a net capital amount which represents investment expenditures that could have been consumed without reducing sustainable consumption per person. Unlike the original ISEW, this takes account of technological progress and assumes trend total factor productivity growth at 1.25 per cent per year in line with the estimates in Crafts and O'Mahony (2001). Obviously, someone who believes that the New Economy will transform growth prospects would have an even larger net capital entry for 1998. ISEW includes a value for non-market work, i.e. the production of goods and services by households for themselves. This is retained. ISEW does not include gains from longer life expectancy, which are added in to revised ISEW using the methodology underlying Table 7.

The negatives in Table 9 are all retained unaltered from the original ISEW estimates in Jackson *et al.* (1997), who provide details of the assumptions on which they are based. As noted above, these have not been re-examined and may deserve revision in future. The revisions to consumption are to deduct items like the cost of commuting which, it is argued, should be treated as an intermediate good rather than final consumption. Pollution and environmental damage impose costs on consumers that are not recognised by the national accounts, and depreciation of natural capital takes account *inter alia* of the depletion of non-renewable energy resources.

3 EXPLORING LONG-RUN GROWTH POTENTIAL

In this chapter further details of long-run economic perform-ance are discussed. Here the focus is not on economic growth *per se* but on other characteristics of British economic development as-sociated with long-run growth potential. Some of these features, such as shares of trade and patenting, are best regarded as diag-nostics which can perhaps reveal something of the strengths and weaknesses of productivity performance but are not themselves policy objectives or direct measures of economic welfare.

This chapter also examines trends in the 'proximate determi-nants' of growth, using the traditional tools of growth accounting pioneered by Denison (1967). This provides insight into the sources of growth and thus both into why growth rates have dif-fered and whether such differences are likely to continue. This level of explanation deals only with the ways in which growth has been achieved; it does not deal with the more profound issues of what caused levels of investment or rates of productivity advance, nor with the reasons for management behaviour or political deci-sions that might influence these variables.

Table 10 reports a decline in Britain's share of world export trade in manufactures from 30.9 per cent in 1913 to 8.8 per cent in 1997. The decline in world market share is shown to have been ex-ceptionally rapid between 1950 and 1973. This is slightly mislead-ing for two reasons: (i) in 1950 British world market share was

Table 10 **Shares of manufactured exports (per cent)**

	1913	1950	1973	1997
Belgium	5.1	6.4	6.7	5.1
Canada	0.6	6.3	5.0	5.5
France	12.4	9.9	9.6	8.8
Germany	27.3	7.2	22.2	17.4
Italy	3.4	3.7	6.8	8.3
Japan	2.4	3.5	12.8	15.6
Netherlands	n/a	3.0	5.1	4.4
Sweden	1.4	2.9	3.4	2.8
Switzerland	3.2	4.2	3.2	2.8
UK	30.9	25.4	9.1	8.8
USA	13.3	27.5	16.1	20.4

Sources: Maizels (1963), Central Statistical Office (1992) and United Nations (1999).
Percentages are based on the countries shown in the table rather than total world
exports. Figures for Germany refer to West Germany in 1950 and 1973.

distorted by the aftermath of the war – in 1937 it was only 20.9 per
cent; (ii) the market shares relate only to the countries in the table
and, since 1973, they have collectively lost considerable ground to
newly industrialising countries.

Again, these data on world market shares are principally of interest as diagnostics. In fact, effective analysis of trade performance requires more detailed information on its correlates at the
sectoral level. This suggests that British exporting success prior to
World War I depended on traditional staples such as textiles and
was not based on high-tech sectors that were research or high-
skilled labour intensive. In other words, Britain was a very different leader in world trade from the United States after World War
II (Crafts and Thomas, 1986; Crafts, 1989).

Since the war, the pattern of comparative advantage revealed
in Britain's trade has changed completely so that in recent years
relatively strong trade performance is positively correlated with

Table 11 **Patents granted in the USA, 1883–1997 (per cent all foreign patenting)**

	1883	1913	1938	1950	1973	1997
Australia	1.1	2.0	1.2	1.5	0.9	1.3
Austria	2.6	4.0	2.9	0.5	1.0	0.7
Belgium	1.6	1.3	1.2	1.1	1.2	0.9
Canada	19.9	13.2	6.4	11.2	6.2	4.6
Denmark	0.6	0.7	0.7	1.4	0.7	0.9
France	14.2	8.1	9.2	15.5	9.4	5.5
Germany	18.7	34.0	38.2	0.6	24.2	14.7
Italy	0.2	1.3	1.4	0.9	3.4	2.3
Japan	0.2	0.4	1.5	0	22.1	39.5
Netherlands	0.2	0.5	3.4	8.1	3.0	2.0
Norway	0.3	0.7	0.5	1.0	0.4	0.4
South Korea	0	0	0	0	0	4.6
Sweden	1.0	2.1	3.1	6.7	3.4	2.7
Switzerland	1.8	3.1	3.7	9.7	5.8	2.0
UK	34.6	23.3	22.7	36.0	12.6	6.5
Others	3.0	5.3	3.9	5.8	5.7	11.4

Sources: Pavitt and Soete (1982); OECD (1999a).

research intensiveness and skilled workforces (Owen, 1995). Nevertheless, econometric research has shown clearly that relatively weak innovative efforts and skill formation in Britain have had negative implications for manufactured exports (Greenhalgh, 1990; Oulton, 1996) and the continuing decline in world market share may well echo this.

Innovative activities are also reflected in Table 11, albeit imperfectly. Parallel to the decline in Britain's share of manufactured trade has been a fall in our share of patents in the United States. This was particularly rapid in the period from the late 1950s to the end of the 1970s and has slowed a little subsequently. An even more striking long-run trend is, of course, the rise of Japan to dominance. In 1997, however, the UK still remained the third-largest foreign patenter with success stories like pharmaceuticals.

Although Britain's share of patents in the late nineteenth century was relatively high, it should be remembered that this was in the infancy of modern research and development activities, when expenditure amounted to perhaps 0.1 per cent, rising to perhaps 0.3 to 0.5 per cent of GDP by the 1930s (Edgerton and Horrocks, 1994). By contrast, in the postwar period spending on R & D has been much larger, generally around 2 per cent of GDP since the early 1960s, but has failed in the long run to match that elsewhere or to yield an equivalent impact on productivity (Verspagen, 1996).

While Tables 10 and 11 dealt with symptoms or side effects of the growth process, Tables 12 to 14 focus on aspects of the supply side of the economy which are proximate determinants of economic growth. Table 12 reports on schooling, which is the most widely used measure of human capital formation in comparative analyses of economic growth. Two points stand out here. First, in the long run, years of schooling have grown at more or less the same rate in most advanced countries. Second, as with R & D, it is striking that in the modern world the UK invests far more in formal education than it did in the nineteenth century.

Despite the attention regularly given to schooling in cross-section studies of growth, it may not be the most important aspect of human capital but simply the most easily measured. Broadberry and Wagner (1996) pointed to a substantial lag in the proportion of top management with degree-level education compared with the United States from at least the 1920s onward. They also stressed that, since World War II, apprenticeship has declined in British manufacturing compared with Germany, which also developed a much larger stock of workers with intermediate vocational qualifications.

Table 12 **Average years of schooling of the labour force**

	1870	1913	1950	1973	1998
Belgium			8.6	10.0	10.8
France		6.2	8.2	9.6	10.6
Germany		6.9	8.5	9.3	13.6
Ireland			9.0	9.8	10.3
Italy			4.9	6.6	9.8
Japan		5.1	8.1	10.2	12.0
Netherlands		6.0	7.6	8.9	11.8
Portugal			2.3	4.0	7.7
South Korea			3.4	5.8	10.8
Spain			5.0	5.4	8.6
Sweden			8.4	9.0	11.6
Taiwan			3.6	5.9	8.7
UK	4.2	7.3	9.4	10.2	12.0
USA		6.9	9.5	11.8	12.7

Sources: Col. 1: Matthews *et al.* (1982); col. 2: Maddison (1991); col. 3: Maddison (1989, 1996); col. 4: Maddison (1996); col. 5: Bassanini *et al.* (2001); South Korea and Taiwan in cols 4 and 5 from Barro and Lee (2000).

In the last twenty years, the skill level of British workers as measured by qualifications has improved but has not caught up with countries like Germany. In 1978/79, 21.8 per cent of the British labour force possessed intermediate and 6.8 per cent higher-level qualifications compared with 58.5 per cent and 7.0 per cent, respectively, in West Germany. By 1998, the proportions with intermediate and higher qualifications in Britain had risen to 34.6 per cent and 16.6 per cent respectively, while in Germany the shares were 63.8 per cent and 13.5 per cent (Crafts and O'Mahony, 2001).

Table 13 reports estimates of the share of GDP devoted to non-residential investment, that is, to physical capital accumulation. Again it is clear that the UK now invests much more than in the nineteenth century. In the Golden Age the UK had the second-lowest investment rate, however, and there has

Table 13 **Gross non-residential investment (per cent GDP)**

	1870–1913	1930–8	1960–73	1980–99
Australia	11.7	10.8	20.2	18.2
Austria			21.1	18.2
Belgium			16.5	18.4
Canada	13.4	10.4	16.9	14.3
Denmark			16.5	13.7
Finland			20.0	16.2
France	10.1	12.1	16.3	14.6
Germany	12.9	9.8	19.6	14.8
Ireland			16.1	14.4
Italy			16.6	14.4
Japan	13.1	13.6	26.5	23.7
Netherlands		14.0	19.8	14.9
South Korea			16.6	26.0
Spain			17.9	16.5
Sweden			16.8	13.9
Taiwan			16.6	19.7
UK	6.9	6.0	14.6	13.7
USA	10.4	9.8	13.5	14.1

Sources: Bank of Korea, Monthly Statistical Bulletin (various issues), van de Klundert and van Schaik (1996), OECD (2000b) and Republic of China (1999). Figures for Taiwan in col. 4. are for 1980–97.

been no improvement since 1980. In both periods, however, the gap with the median country is fairly small.

While capital accumulation does promote growth, it is also true that investment responds to growth opportunities. Indeed, in general the second linkage is probably stronger than the first (Blomstrom *et al.*, 1996). It is not particularly surprising, then, that the UK, with less scope for catch-up than elsewhere, was not among the countries with the highest investment rates in the early postwar years. By the same token, however, the relatively low level of investment argues against a dramatic transformation in British growth prospects since 1980.

Labour productivity growth is influenced by many variables, but the main proximate ones are capital accumulation, acquisition of skills, technological progress, scale economies and better utilisation of resources. It is desirable to quantify these contributions, and growth accounting techniques (which are briefly described below, but see Barro (1999) for a full exposition) offer one way of doing this. It is also very important to try to distinguish between transitory and long-lasting sources of productivity growth. This requires theoretical insights as well as careful measurement.

Table 14 reports growth accounting calculations from Maddison (1991, 1996), which are the best available for the long run. The sources of growth are divided into growth of total factor inputs and of total factor productivity (TFP). The former measures the contributions of increases in the available factors of production, taking account both of quantity and quality; two aspects of this (non-residential capital accumulation and education of the labour force) are highlighted in the table – other items are not shown. Embodied technological progress will be reflected in new types and/or enhanced quality of physical capital. Evidence relating to the responsiveness of output to additional factor inputs can be used to weight the relative importance of growth in labour and capital inputs. Recent research tends to confirm that weights of about 0.7 and 0.3 respectively are appropriate (Oulton and Young, 1996).

TFP growth stems from increases in output over and above those resulting from additional capital and labour and is generated by better resource allocation, disembodied technological progress and more intensive use of factors of production. To the extent that improvements in the quality of labour and capital are under (over)-estimated, TFP will be over (under)-estimated. In

Table 14 **Accounting for sources of long-run growth (per cent per year)**

	France	Germany	Japan	UK	USA
1913–50					
GDP	1.15	1.28	2.24	1.29	2.79
Total factor input	0.48	1.00	1.57	0.94	1.53
Non-residential capital	0.63	0.59	1.23	0.72	0.81
Education	0.36	0.24	0.61	0.33	0.41
Total factor productivity	0.67	0.28	0.67	0.35	1.26
Catch-up effect	0.00	0.00	0.00	0.00	0.00
Foreign trade effect	0.03	-0.13	0.05	0.01	0.04
Structural effect	0.04	0.20	0.40	-0.04	0.29
Scale effect	0.03	0.04	0.07	0.04	0.08
Unexplained	0.57	0.17	0.15	0.34	0.85
1950–73					
GDP	5.02	5.99	9.25	2.96	3.91
Total factor input	1.96	2.71	5.63	1.71	2.34
Non-residential capital	1.59	2.20	3.06	1.64	1.05
Education	0.36	0.19	0.52	0.18	0.48
Total factor productivity	3.06	3.28	3.62	1.25	1.57
Catch-up effect	0.46	0.62	0.98	0.08	0.00
Foreign trade effect	0.37	0.48	0.53	0.32	0.11
Structural effect	0.36	0.36	1.22	0.10	0.10
Scale effect	0.15	0.18	0.28	0.09	0.12
Unexplained	1.72	1.64	0.61	0.66	1.24
1973–92					
GDP	2.26	2.30	3.76	1.59	2.39
Total factor input	1.61	0.77	2.55	0.96	2.22
Non-residential capital	1.26	0.93	1.97	0.93	0.90
Education	0.67	0.11	0.26	0.43	0.46
Total factor productivity	0.65	1.53	1.21	0.63	0.17
Catch-up effect	0.31	0.31	0.39	0.20	0.00
Foreign trade effect	0.12	0.15	0.09	0.15	0.05
Structural effect	0.15	0.17	0.20	-0.09	-0.17
Scale effect	0.07	0.07	0.11	0.05	0.07
Unexplained	0.00	0.83	0.42	0.32	0.22

Sources: Derived from Maddison (1991, 1996).

Table 14 Maddison's attempts to identify the components of TFP growth are split into five components, the last of which, 'unexplained', is essentially a combination of the acquisition and effective use of knowledge and measurement error.

Some of the sources of growth identified in Table 14 are largely once-and-for-all rather than likely to be sustained indefinitely. This is probably true of the first three components of TFP growth. Catch-up effects come from reducing the productivity gap with the leading country and will tend to peter out in mature economies. The next two (foreign trade and structural) effects refer to the improved use of resources associated with trade liberalisation and the run-down of low productivity sectors like traditional agriculture, which are also inherently limited in their scope.

Table 15 reports further, less refined, estimates of TFP growth for the business sector only. These show higher rates of TFP growth because they leave out the government sector and because they do not adjust labour or capital inputs for quality. Their advantage is their wider country coverage. In these estimates, the UK's late Golden Age TFP growth is about average, but below the fast-growing western European countries. In the last two decades, as other countries experienced a sharp slowdown, TFP growth in the UK slowed less than most, and the UK moved up to third in the table. To a significant extent, this probably reflects improvements in the quality of the labour force, especially as the proportion of manual employment has fallen markedly, rather than above-average performance in innovation.

Perhaps less obviously, it should also be recognised that, in the absence of technological progress, a higher investment rate will also have only a transitory effect on growth. Given that there are diminishing returns to routine capital accumulation (Oulton and

Table 15 **Total factor productivity (tfp) growth in the business sector (per cent per year)**

	1960–73			1980–98	
1	Japan	5.4	1	Ireland	3.4
	Portugal	5.4	2	Finland	2.5
3	Ireland	4.6	3	UK	1.6
4	Italy	4.4	4	Australia	1.4
5	Finland	4.0	5	Denmark	1.3
6	Belgium	3.8		Portugal	1.3
7	France	3.7		Sweden	1.3
8	Netherlands	3.4	8	France	1.2
9	Spain	3.2		Italy	1.2
10	Austria	3.1		Japan	1.2
11	Germany	2.6	11	Germany	1.1
	UK	2.6		Netherlands	1.1
13	Greece	2.5		Norway	1.1
	USA	2.5		Spain	1.1
15	Denmark	2.3	15	Belgium	0.9
16	Australia	2.2		USA	0.9
17	Switzerland	2.1	17	Austria	0.8
18	Norway	2.0	18	Canada	0.5
	Sweden	2.0	19	Greece	0.2
20	Canada	1.9	20	Switzerland	0.0

Source: Scarpetta et al. (2000).

Young, 1996), in the long run, the impact of a rise in the investment rate on growth of the capital stock is offset by a rising capital-to-output ratio. Even the initial impact of a 1 percentage point rise in the investment rate is fairly modest – probably about 0.2 percentage points on the growth rate based on the growth accounting arithmetic. The key to sustained increases in the long-run growth rate is a higher rate of innovation, rather than accumulating ever-larger quantities of the same capital equipment.

Obviously, the growth accounting approach is demanding of data, is potentially vulnerable to measurement problems, and poses some problems of interpretation (Crafts and O'Mahony, 2001). Nevertheless, it is a useful way of benchmarking performance and several important messages can be extracted from Tables 14 and 15 which are probably quite robust.

- Very rapid growth in OECD countries was accompanied by strong TFP growth; the slowdown in growth since 1973 in previously fast-growth countries has come both from capital's contribution and from TFP but much more from the latter.
- Transitory components of TFP growth were unusually high in the fast-growth countries during the Golden Age and then slowed. In fact, alternative methods of implementing growth accounting suggest that this point may be understated by Table 14 (Crafts, 1995).
- During the period of rapid relative economic decline in the Golden Age, the shortfall in British growth came substantially from TFP growth. Some of this was attributable to less scope for rapid transitory TFP growth at the start of the period, but there may well have been a substantial failure in the effective application of new knowledge. In any event, there is an 'unexplained' shortfall in TFP growth of around 1 per cent per year.
- There is nothing in recent TFP growth to suggest that growth potential in the UK is higher than in the Golden Age; on the contrary, the opposite seems clearly to be the case.

The big picture that has been built up in this chapter comprises the following elements. First, relative economic decline has stemmed from weak productivity performance rather than simply from low investment. Second, a wide range of indicators is suggestive of a relatively weak capacity for successful innovation lying at the heart of relative decline. Third, the growth potential of the economy in recent decades is well above that of a century ago; the UK has improved absolutely since then but other countries have taken better advantage of increased growth opportunities.

4 AN INTERPRETATION OF RELATIVE DECLINE FROM 1870 TO THE 1970S

Chapter 1 provided some essential background with which to approach the interpretation of British growth performance. Several important points were established, including:

- incentive structures affect productivity outcomes through their impact both on investment decisions and on the politicians' willingness to sacrifice long-run growth for short-term electoral advantage;
- supply-side policy has varied a great deal, ranging from near laissez-faire prior to 1914 to a high point of state intervention in the 1970s;
- broadly speaking, industrial policy is more likely to stimulate growth when companies are profit-maximising but competition policy will be more effective when firms are subject to agency problems (Figure 1);
- a consensus on Britain's 'failure' has not been reached, not least because competing claims have deep political roots.

From the literature review, it also became clear that the major issue arising is the extent to which government failure or market failure has been responsible for Britain's relative economic decline.

Catch-up growth

It was noted earlier that, given social capability and technological congruence, rapid growth can be achieved in periods of catch-up. This idea now needs to be put in the context of a more general view of economic growth and the forces for convergence or divergence in the OECD countries. The following summary draws on the more extensive discussions in Crafts (1998, 1999). There are three key points.

First, catch-up is not automatic, nor does it necessarily lead to complete convergence. Catching up is based on having in place appropriate institutions and policies to facilitate investment, innovation and technology transfer, and also to prevent vested interests from obstructing the growth process. Econometric research suggests both that the experience of leading economies is not consistent with the view that productivity levels are tending to equalisation and that countries differ in their labour productivity levels by a lot more than would be expected simply on the basis of their investment in human and physical capital. This is because their economies are organised on the basis of varying degrees of inefficiency and/or because technology does not always transfer easily. In other words, there is room to succeed or to fail, and differences in scope for catch-up are a conditioning rather than a determining factor in growth.

Second, it is not always possible or desirable to adopt other countries' technology, and this may be a reason for persistent divergence in income or productivity levels which does not connote failure. Countries differ in terms of their factor endowments and cost conditions, so that techniques discovered and adopted in one location may not be economically rational elsewhere. Moreover, much technological knowledge is 'tacit' and is a product of experience in the form of localised learning of 'know-how' rather than 'know-why' and not readily communicated or employed in foreign parts.

Third, in successful countries economic growth in the twentieth century was much faster than in the nineteenth century, in particular through unprecedented TFP growth. Britain in the Industrial Revolution should be seen as an economy whose achievements, based on an early embrace of capitalism and comparative advantage, were hugely impressive compared with what had gone before but whose growth potential was very limited by later standards. The economy invested less than 10 per cent of GDP, only about half the labour force was literate, and, notwithstanding spectacular technological advances in textiles and steam power, TFP growth was less than 0.5 per cent per year. From today's perspective, it is striking how much effort was directed towards rent-seeking and warfare rather than productive entrepreneurship and education, how weak were the incentives for innovation, and how primitive was the legal infrastructure underpinning company and capital market organisation. To catch up, once overtaken by the United States in the late nineteenth century, Britain would need to adapt and to modernise.

American overtaking before World War II

Bearing these points in mind, relative economic decline prior to World War II can be examined. Broadly speaking, the major shortfall in British performance at this time was relative to the United States rather than Europe, and this will be the focal point of the following discussion. Table 5 showed an already large gap in labour productivity in industry in 1870 which widened substantially thereafter; by 1950 the United States was also well ahead in labour productivity in agriculture and services. The most important reasons for this productivity gap with the United States stem from factor endowments enhanced by international factor flows.

In 1870 the USA was a large and still relatively empty country amply endowed with natural resources which underpinned high output (and wages) per worker. This attracted mass immigration and foreign investment. Although in a simple neoclassical model this might have promoted a shift from agriculture to manufacturing, accompanied by convergence of wages and labour productivity (Lewis, 1979; O'Rourke and Williamson, 1994), in the presence of economies of scale, both internal and external, in manufacturing, the rapidly growing size of the American economy, which became far larger than any of its European rivals, sustained the initial wage gap with the UK and facilitated overtaking in real GDP per person (Crafts and Venables, 2001).

Technological progress also played an important part in the American overtaking of Britain. Partly this was due to the pattern of comparative advantage, which pushed Britain away from and the United States towards sectors with high TFP growth potential in the early twentieth century (Thomas, 1988). Partly it came from trajectories of technical change based on cheap natural resources and mass markets which in turn underwrote an expansion of college education and encouraged R & D. Even in the late nineteenth century, productivity growth was modest; TFP growth in both the UK and the USA was around 0.5 per cent per year (Abramovitz, 1993; Matthews *et al.*, 1982), but in the early twentieth century the United States moved to a faster growth path based on much greater technological prowess and economic scale than hitherto.

Table 14 reports American TFP growth of 1.26 per cent per year for 1913–50.

These developments were difficult for Europeans to emulate – in large part for reasons beyond their control. The technological learning that accumulated in the United States was hard to transfer and often of limited relevance in European conditions (Nelson and Wright, 1992). In manufacturing, large markets permitted more scale economies while encouraging the development of large corporations and greater R & D whose fixed costs could be spread over a larger volume of sales. In the services sector, American productivity advance was founded on the development of new hierarchical forms of organisation based on large volumes and reduced costs of monitoring workers as communication costs fell (Broadberry and Ghosal, 2000). This was a new world quite unlike that of the Industrial Revolution.

Even so, was American overtaking aided and abetted by market failure in Britain? Two claims need to be examined, those of 'entrepreneurial failure' and of 'capital market failure'. The former no longer commands much support since, on the whole, these charges have been refuted. As Pollard concluded: 'British industry was an open, highly competitive world. Entrepreneurial failure would imply the simultaneous failure of thousands of individuals ... plus the failure of thousands more who were eagerly waiting to take their places if they failed. Such a development would surely strain credulity beyond reason' (1994: 79).

Detailed microeconomic studies have shown that, although British managers often did not adopt American methods, their decisions were generally rational given British conditions in which the cost of skilled labour was lower and that of natural resources higher and existing arrangements often facilitated efficient production. For example, the cotton industry was not disadvantaged by its alleged failure to integrate spinning and weaving but benefited from atomistic competition in thick markets and from substantial external economies of scale that allowed it to survive in the face of low wage competition from abroad (Broadberry and Marrison, 2002; Leunig, 2001). When Ford moved to Britain it soon recognised that Fordist methods geared to assimilating unskilled immigrants in a different tradition of industrial relations were not appropriate in British conditions (Lewchuk, 1989). Similarly, the slower move to corporate capitalism in the UK was responsible for, at most, only a small part of the manufacturing productivity gap with the United States (Broadberry and Crafts, 1992).

The issues regarding capital market failure are rather more complex. At one level, the market was highly efficient. The detailed econometric investigation by Edelstein (1976) showed that there were few apparent inefficiencies in capital allocation and, in particular, that foreign investment was not unduly favoured and that the *ex post* rate of return on new industries lagged behind that of traditional sectors between 1870 and 1913. Michie (1988) pointed to the ease with which the fledgling motor industry could raise money through public issues and argued that this indicated that the capital market was not over-committed to traditional industries.

Nevertheless, to modern eyes there were serious weaknesses in Victorian company law that must have impaired both company flotations and dealing with agency problems within firms. Among the deficiencies were the delay in compulsory auditing of most limited liability joint stock companies until 1900, in requiring publication of profit-and-loss accounts until 1929, and in preventing the use of secret reserves to distort trading results until 1948. It was not until the Companies Act of that year that adequate disclosure requirements were introduced and auditors were placed under a duty to report whether the accounts were true and fair (Edwards, 1989). Shareholders required greater protection from unscrupulous company promoters if the market for new issues was to work effectively, and econometric analysis suggests that deficiencies in company legislation had an adverse effect on both the volume and efficiency of investment (Foreman-Peck, 1990).

Hannah described the situation prior to 1948 as 'a golden age of directorial power' (1974: 77) in which shareholders were unable effectively to monitor and where hostile takeovers could not effectively discipline management. Thus, where there was failure to perform adequately, the economy lacked effective mechanisms to remove inefficient firms and managers. This made the experience of the 1930s, when the British policy response to the depression was to reduce the competitive pressure on firms, especially unfortunate.

Faced with world deflation, the coalition government of the 1930s pursued a 'managed economy' strategy to restore profitability by raising prices relative to wages (Booth, 1987). This included devaluation, restriction of capital exports, encouraging cartels and collusive behaviour, and imposing a general tariff on manufactures in 1932. Both case study and econometric evidence reveal that this switch of policy was damaging to productivity performance (Broadberry and Crafts, 1992). In this protected environment it is not surprising to read in a survey of business histories that 'even large companies retained a cosy amateurishness' (Gourvish, 1987: 34) and to find that many of them appear to have responded inadequately to strategic opportunities (Hannah, 1983).

If relative economic decline prior to World War II was largely unavoidable, there were warning signs by the 1930s to the effect that the direction of government policy was likely to have unfortunate consequences for long-run productivity performance by eliminating competition in an economy that lacked adequate mechanisms for preventing persistent managerial failure. With an increasing divorce of ownership and control and bigger barriers to entry, the 1930s were some considerable distance removed from the competitive environment that had restrained Victorian entrepreneurial failure.

Falling behind in the Golden Age

The experience of the 1950s up until the 1970s, when Britain was overtaken by so many European countries, was rather different. In this period, although the UK grew faster than at any time in its history, the verdict must be one of opportunities missed. Key features of the early postwar British economy were the increasingly damaging system of industrial relations, the decline of traditional vocational training, and the weakness of competition. The following discussion draws on the more detailed treatment in Bean and Crafts (1996).

In the postwar period, the possibilities for catch-up growth were much greater than previously, but to exploit these circumstances fully it was necessary to have appropriate institutions and to make the right policy choices. Technology transfer was enhanced by the further spread of multinational companies, the growing integration of markets, investments in higher education and R & D, and the increased codification of technological knowledge with the result that Europe (and Japan) could rapidly narrow the large mid-century productivity gap with the USA (Nelson and Wright, 1992). The lack of technological congruence that had impeded European catch-up of the United States in the early twentieth century evaporated.

More stable macroeconomic conditions, trade liberalisation and the repairing of the damage caused by depression and war promoted structural change and rapid recovery. At the same time, the reconstruction of European economies generally succeeded in reforming relationships between capital and labour in ways that encouraged high investment in return for wage moderation (Eichengreen, 1996). For fast-growing European economies, rapid TFP growth and a much-strengthened contribution to growth from capital accumulation were the outcome. The UK clearly did develop a higher growth potential in the postwar world but did not take full advantage of the situation. Even allowing for lower scope for catch-up, European experience suggests that a growth rate of 0.75 to 1 per cent per year faster was surely possible.

Britain did not achieve the transformation in industrial relations that happened elsewhere in Europe and remained an outlier, the only case of powerful, long-established but decentralised trade unionism (Crouch, 1993). The British system was characterised by multiple unionism, unenforceable contracts and, increasingly, by plant bargaining with shop stewards, while with full employment and relatively weak competition in product markets workers' bargaining power was strong. The evidence suggests that this environment in which, unlike in countries such as Germany, workers and firms could not commit themselves to 'good behaviour', seriously weakened incentives to investment and innovation (Bean and Crafts, 1996; Denny and Nickell, 1992).

Vocational training in early postwar Britain left a lot to be desired and fell behind other European countries like Germany which had also continued to specialise in craft production rather than adopt the Fordist methods of the United States. Whereas just prior to World War I apprentices accounted for 15 per cent of employment in the engineering industries in Britain compared with 10 per cent in Germany, in the 1950s the proportions were 4 per cent in Britain and 8 per cent in Germany (Broadberry and Wagner, 1996). Unlike its German counterpart, British industry did not develop a set of (corporatist) institutions based on internal labour markets and employers' organisations to internalise training externalities, both by making it worthwhile for juveniles to train and by eliminating the classic poaching problem (Soskice, 1994). The main government policy response in the form of the Industrial Training Act of 1964 was both belated and ineffective (Vickerstaff, 1985).

Cartelisation, which had proliferated during the 1930s and 1940s, characterised the greater part of the manufacturing sector and was correlated with poor productivity performance as the exit of inefficient plant was slowed down and incentives to innovate were diluted (Broadberry and Crafts, 2001; Elliott and Gribbin, 1977). The absence of competition in much of the economy was initially reinforced by the legacy of inter-war protectionism and then, as Owen (1999) has emphasised, by turning down the opportunity to join the European Economic Community in 1957. This was particularly unfortunate because there are reasons to think that agency problems were pervasive in British industry at this time.

First, econometric analysis has found that in the 1970s and 1980s greater (though not perfect) competition promoted innovation (Blundell *et al.*, 1999; Geroski, 1990) and raised productivity growth where companies did not have a dominant external shareholder (Nickell *et al.*, 1997). In this (typical) case a fall of supernormal profits from 15 to 5 per cent of value-added raised TFP growth by 1 percentage point per year, and financial pressure raised productivity growth, especially where competition was weak. When rents were 25 per cent of value-added a rise in interest payments from 10 to 30 per cent of cash flow raised productivity growth by 1.7 per cent per year – so subsidies, by easing cash flow problems, would have undermined cost-reducing effort.

Second, case studies found that lack of competition also seems to have resulted in a situation where managers did not pursue cost reductions assiduously and workers bargained a share of the rents into overstaffing; inefficient use of labour and complacent management are pervasive themes in investigations from the 1950s up until the 1970s (Pratten and Atkinson, 1976). This conclusion is reinforced by the role that increased competition played in the shake-out of manufacturing jobs in the 1980s (Haskel, 1991).

Third, although the 1948 Companies Act increased the possibilities for hostile takeovers, it did not lead to a world in which management was effectively disciplined as shareholding was too diffuse and institutional shareholders did not act generally as an effective check. A well-documented case of shareholder failure to remove inadequate management is that of Morris Motors (Bowden *et al.*, 2001). Changes in the capital market did by the 1960s encourage a ferocious merger and takeover boom, but one in which size rather than efficiency or long-term investment determined survival (Singh, 1975). The evidence suggests that mergers were not generally associated with productivity gains (Meeks, 1977) but were the result of management pursuing its own objectives rather than the interests of the shareholders (Newbould, 1970).

Fourth, productivity performance and return on assets in nationalised industries were deeply disappointing (Vickers and Yarrow, 1988). By the 1970s this had been clearly linked to inadequate monitoring and control, together with the use of state-owned enterprise for political rather than economic purposes. NEDO (1976) underlined the lack of accountability and incentives for management, together with the absence of effective systems of performance measurement.

Policy errors and institutional failings became more costly in this new environment of rapid catch-up growth than they had been in the inter-war period. Immediately after the war, economic policy options were severely circumscribed by the legacy of repressed inflation and balance of payments problems which, for example, seriously compromised attempts to inject greater competition into the economy and thus weakened productivity performance (Broadberry and Crafts, 1996). Subsequently, however, during the Golden Age, there was a great deal of experimentation in economic policy-making involving efforts to enhance productivity growth as well as to reduce economic insecurity and inequality.

Supply-side policy did not, however, focus effectively on addressing market failures in human capital formation or the diffusion of technical knowledge. Instead, the thrust of policy was to subsidise physical capital, to nationalise and/or not to privatise, to finance prestige research projects, notably in aerospace and nuclear power, to promote 'national champion' firms, and to maintain a highly distortionary tax system. Industrial policy was generally a much higher priority than competition policy, although the 1956 Restrictive Practices Act did lead to the demise of most cartels.

In addition, the electoral importance that was attached to

short-run macroeconomic outcomes such as unemployment and inflation was a major constraint on policy. This led successive governments to seek (often informal) 'social contracts' with organised labour in which the desire for wage moderation in effect implied that there were no-go areas in microeconomic policy. Most obviously, this precluded reform of the system of industrial relations, but it was also an obstacle to tax reform and to allowing the process of creative destruction to promote productivity growth.

The evidence regarding the interventionist policies of the 1970s is that they slowed down much-needed structural adjustment. The picture is that 'it was losers like Rolls Royce, British Leyland and Alfred Herbert who picked Ministers ... What was described as "picking winners" appeared in practice to amount to spending huge sums shoring up ailing companies ... ' (Morris and Stout, 1985: 873). For example, government contributions to civil aircraft and engine development from 1945 to 1974 totalled £1.5 billion at 1974 prices and produced receipts of £0.14 billion (Gardner, 1976). Similarly, Greenaway and Milner (1994) concluded that the pattern of protection in the form of tariffs in the UK in 1979 was primarily accounted for in terms of the adjustment costs associated with threatened contraction of industries with high import penetration and intense use of unskilled labour.

It seems clear that the importance of agency problems for policy design was not well understood. This is most clearly seen in the choice of nationalisation rather than regulation as the policy regime to deal with market failure in the infrastructure industries (Millward, 1997). It is also evident, however, in the naive Schumpeterian beliefs that informed competition policy in the early postwar period (Broadberry and Crafts, 2001).

To some extent, similar policy errors were made throughout

Europe, but overall the damage done in Britain was relatively high, as international comparisons have often shown. Thus, Tanzi (1969) concluded that the British tax system was the least conducive to growth of any OECD country that he studied, Adams (1989) found that early entry into the European Community provided an antidote to misdirected industrial policies absent in Britain, Kormendi and Meguire (1985) obtained econometric results to show that unpredictable macroeconomic policies hurt growth in the UK more than in any other major European economy, while Ergas (1987) contrasted the success of Germany's technology policy in speeding up diffusion with the failure of the invention-oriented British policy.

Concluding comments

Lack of technological congruence and social capability are fundamental reasons for falling behind and obstacles to catching up. Britain's productivity gap with the United States before World War II was largely a result of the former, while the failure to catch up as rapidly as other European countries in the postwar period was mainly due to the latter. Prior to 1914 Britain lacked America's natural resources. After 1945 Britain suffered from incentive structures that had adverse effects on investment, innovation and policy-making.

The American overtaking of Britain was unavoidable in the early twentieth century, and market failure was at most a second-order problem. Capital market institutions were not, however, conducive to exploiting fully the potential of creative destruction for productivity performance. Government failures were of omission rather than commission, but these were probably no worse than those evident in other countries. In particular, recent research has tended to take a much more favourable view of educational policy; Sanderson's review concluded that 'the British system of education was so transformed ... between 1890 and 1914 that it had become an impressive support for industry rather than a liability' (1999: 26).

The European overtaking of Britain in the 1960s and 1970s was not inevitable. Market failures permitted low-effort equilibria, characterised by managerial self-indulgence and under-utilisation of labour inputs, to persist. Institutional failures in the areas of industrial relations and vocational training were not self-correcting. The message that in such circumstances a strong emphasis should be placed on strengthening competition rather than on industrial policy was not understood and/or was too uncomfortable to act upon. This was a period of significant government failure. The evidence does not suggest that the government should have done more but rather less in the way of seeking to influence the allocation of capital.

Government failure in the decades after World War II can be accounted for in three ways. First, inadequate theory plus lack of experience of the effects of state intervention led to badly designed policies – for example, extensive nationalisation. Second, the perceived need to win votes by taking responsibility for achieving good short-term macroeconomic outcomes precluded necessary supply-side reforms – for example, in industrial relations. Third, there was too much discretion available to governments which could not commit themselves to policies that tied their hands in the face of interest-group pressures to delay restructuring or exit by firms, as was made strikingly apparent by the U-turns of the Heath government in the early 1970s.

5 SUCCESS OR FAILURE SINCE 1979?

The election of the Thatcher government in 1979 marked the start of a new approach to reversing relative economic decline and improving 'competitiveness' which has largely been sustained by the Labour government since 1997. Among the key elements of the new supply-side policy have been privatisation and deregulation, downsizing of industrial policy, reform of industrial relations, restructuring of taxation and restraint on the growth of public expenditure, radical revision of vocational training and expansion of higher education. Foreign direct investment has been encouraged and rapid deindustrialisation more or less accepted.

Many of these policies would have been inconceivable to earlier Conservative governments, let alone the 'Old' Labour governments of Attlee, Callaghan and Wilson. In principle, leaving aside details of implementation, the revised policy stance would be consistent with the insights of modern growth economics, especially if agency problems are prevalent. The task of this chapter is to assess the impact of these reforms on relative productivity performance and its determinants. In particular, it will be important to consider how far major obstacles to better productivity performance in the early postwar period – notably, inadequate business management stemming from agency problems, damaging industrial relations, inferior human capital formation, and poor design of supply-side policy – have been overcome.

Progress since the Golden Age

Table 16 (on the following page) places British productivity performance in a comparative context. The main message appears to be that since 1979 relative decline compared with France and Germany, which had been rapid previously, has ceased but has not been substantially reversed. Catch-up with the United States has continued, at least until the last few years. Japanese catch-up with the UK in terms of TFP has faltered. This relatively better showing has come about through a markedly greater slowdown in France, Germany and Japan since the Golden Age rather than an acceleration in UK productivity growth. Capital per worker in the UK in 1999 remained well below the levels in the other countries. None of this should come as a surprise given the evidence set out in Chapter 2.

Table 17 (on page 87) looks much more closely at comparative TFP performance in an attempt to identify the sources of the continuing productivity gap. This is accomplished by working with various concepts of TFP. TFP1 takes into account the use only of physical capital relating to ICT (Information and Communications Technology). TFP2, which is taken from Table 16, is the standard basic concept which includes all physical capital but takes no account of human capital (and is therefore cruder than Maddison's estimates reported in Table 14). TFP3 allows also for labour force skills based on the usual methodology of weighting qualifications by their associated wage differentials. TFP4 additionally takes explicit account of innovation in the form of stocks of R & D and an estimate of their contribution to output growth.

Table 17 reads as follows for 1979. The TFP2 estimate shows that with regard to all three comparator countries a substantial part of the labour productivity gap is attributable to lower

Table 16 **International comparisons of productivity performance, 1950–99**

a) Growth rates of real GDP/hour worked (per cent per year)

	UK	France	Germany	Japan	USA
1950–73					
Total economy	2.99	4.62	5.18	6.11	2.34
1979–99					
Total economy	2.13	2.56	2.39	2.78	1.08

b) Levels of labour productivity, capital intensity and TFP (UK = 100)

	France	Germany	Japan	USA
GDP/hour worked				
1950	76	72	40	190
1973	111	119	77	165
1979	131	130	82	154
1999	124	128	91	126
K/hour worked				
1950	157	135	64	299
1973	142	168	103	174
1979	151	174	109	157
1999	146	145	165	142
TFP				
1950	65	68	50	125
1973	99	104	77	136
1979	114	121	80	132
1999	109	113	77	113

Sources: O'Mahony (1999), updated using Crafts and O'Mahony (2001). Estimates for West Germany in 1999 are approximate.

physical capital per hour worked: 17 out of 31 percentage points, 9 out of 30 and 22 out of 54 compared with France, West Germany and the United States respectively. On top of this, the TFP3 estimate shows that 6 percentage points of the labour productivity

Table 17 **International comparisons of different concepts of total factor productivity (TFP) (UK = 100)**

	France	Germany*	USA
1979			
GDP/HW	131	130	154
TFP1 (ICTK)	n/a	n/a	n/a
TFP2 (K)	114	121	132
TFP3 (K, HK)	108	116	129
TFP4 (K, HK, R&D)	111	111	122
1999			
GDP/HW	124	111	126
TFP1 (ICTK)	128	111	121
TFP2 (K)	109	100	113
TFP3 (K, HK)	105	97	113
TFP4 (K, HK, R&D)	101	100	107

Source: Crafts and O'Mahony (2001).

TFP1 (ICTK) includes only physical capital relating to information and communications technology; TFP2 (K) includes all physical capital; TFP3 (K, HK) includes physical capital and human capital; TFP4 (K, HK, R&D) includes physical capital, human capital and research and development.
* Refers to West Germany in 1979 and unified Germany in 1999.

gap compared with France is accounted for by labour force skills, slightly less in the other two countries. The TFP4 row finds that a further 5 and 7 percentage points of the labour productivity gap come from the impact of R & D in Germany and the United States respectively, but R & D had a larger impact in the UK than in France, so if we take this into account the residual TFP gap has risen 3 percentage points. This bottom line suggests that unexplained TFP differences due to the relative efficiency in the use of factors of production were responsible in 1979 for an 11 percentage point productivity gap with each of France and Germany and a 22 point gap with the United States.

How had this changed by 1999? Now, compared with the

United States none of the labour productivity gap was due to skills, a substantial proportion came from differences in R & D, much as it did in 1979, and there remained a residual efficiency gap which was, however, much lower than in 1979. While the contribution of physical capital overall was lower (Table 16 reports that the capital-to-hour-worked gap fell from 57 to 42 per cent) a new source of productivity advantage for the USA emerged in the shape of higher ICT capital per hour worked, which accounted for 5 of the 26 percentage points gap in GDP/HW.

With respect to France and Germany, physical and human capital were relatively more important than for the USA and R & D less so in explaining the 1999 labour productivity gap. The impact of labour force skills was less than in 1979 but the biggest source of reduction in the GDP/HW gap was in residual TFP. The contribution of physical capital remained large in each case but, interestingly, ICT capital intensity has not lagged in the UK, so the story was not a failure to invest as much in the new economy but rather a weaker record over the longer run of investment in traditional capital.

Table 17 suggests that the most important positive implication of the shift in supply-side policy after 1979 was to improve the efficiency with which factors of production were used. Studies of productivity outcomes have highlighted two areas where this was particularly apparent. Manufacturing has been notable as a sector where, in the 1980s, Thatcherism had a particularly marked impact on productivity performance. Detailed empirical studies suggest that this was associated with a major shake-out relating to stronger competitive pressures and a transformation in industrial relations which eliminated the hold-up problems and overstaffing of the 1970s (Bean and Crafts, 1996; Haskel, 1991; Metcalf, 1994). The average skill level of the workforce improved somewhat as the proportion with no qualifications fell from 72 per cent in 1979 to 54 per cent in 1993 (O'Mahony, 1999). Foreign direct investment, by stimulating technological change, has been estimated to have accounted for about 30 per cent of labour productivity growth between 1985 and 1995 (Barrell and Pain, 1997). However, the important point to remember, as the discussion in Chapter 2 underlined, is that, at the end of the twentieth century, manufacturing was quite a small part of the total economy.

Another much-studied aspect of the recent past has been privatisation, which can also be interpreted as addressing agency problems in British enterprises. Control of managers in the former nationalised industries has been strengthened by privatisation; financial performance had no effect on the probability of top executives resigning or being fired under public ownership, but after several years in the private sector underperforming managers are more commonly being replaced (Cragg and Dyck, 1999). Productivity performance has improved considerably. Twelve of these industries experienced an unweighted average growth rate of real output per worker of 1.3 per cent in 1972–80, rising to 5.6 per cent in 1980–88 and 6.8 per cent in 1988–97 (Europe Economics, 1998).

An unresolved issue is how far the impact of the reforms has impinged on the rate of productivity growth rather than being a one-off effect on its level. Total economy labour productivity growth slowed from 2.3 per cent per year in 1979–89 to 1.9 per cent in 1989–99 and only 1.3 per cent in 1995–9. On a growth accounting basis, contributions from sources other than growth of ICT capital per worker weakened even more (Oulton, 2001). In manufacturing labour productivity stagnated for four years from 1994 to 1998 but then rose by 12 per cent in the next two years.

The answer may partly depend on the extent, as yet unclear, to which the favourable effects of better supply-side policy have been offset by uncertainty over macroeconomic developments. The analysis in Oulton (1995) found that macroeconomic instability had harmed growth performance, presumably through the adverse effects of uncertainty on investment; had macro fluctuations been similar to those in the better-performing countries in the OECD, trend growth could have risen by about 0.5 per cent per year. This suggests that better management of both interest and exchange rate policy could be important in allowing the full benefits of supply-side reform to be realised.

Table 17 also suggests that lack of human capital was a somewhat less important factor in the productivity gap in 1999 than in 1979. There has been quite a rapid change in the composition of the labour force – in 1998 51.2 per cent had higher or intermediate qualifications compared with 28.6 per cent in 1978/79 (Crafts and O'Mahony, 2001). There has also been a substantial increase in the amount of training of those in work; the fraction of workers receiving job-related training in the previous four weeks rose from 8.5 per cent in 1984 to 15.7 per cent in 2000 (Office for National Statistics, 2001) and participation in training ranked third among OECD countries in the 1990s (OECD, 1999b: 142). At the same time, however, the measured skills of young workers seem actually to have fallen relative to older workers. Thus, on OECD measures of competencies in literacy and numeracy, in 1994–8 British 16 to 25-year-olds performed less well than 26 to 35-year-olds, and their average score was fourteenth of fifteen advanced countries tested.

This suggests that while progress has been made on training, critics like Sanderson (1999) are right to worry about the education of less academically able children. Poor-quality schooling is likely to reflect problems of control and management of schools rather than simply levels of expenditure. International evidence suggests that agency problems are very important in the provision of public schooling, and that these are most serious where teacher unions control the curriculum, there are few national examinations and where there is little involvement of the private sector (Wossmann, 2000). These findings support the argument that the general direction of British policy since the late 1980s has made some steps in the right direction but may need to go farther.

Another important influence on the cessation of economic decline relative to Europe can probably be identified in comparative fiscal policies. Recent econometric studies have found that, when the financing aspect of government spending is explicitly taken into account, tax and public investment do influence growth outcomes in the OECD. Broadly speaking, it appears that taxes on income are distortionary and have an adverse impact on growth, whereas taxes on consumption are neutral. Also, productive expenditures by government tend to raise growth whereas transfer payments are neutral. Thus, an increase in, say, unemployment benefits financed by income taxes is growth-reducing whereas higher infrastructure spending financed by higher VAT is growth-enhancing. In both cases a change of 1 per cent of GDP has been estimated to change the growth rate by at least 0.1 percentage point per year (Kneller *et al.*, 1999).

In the light of these results, Tables 18 and 19 (on pages 92 and 93) make interesting reading.

Throughout the OECD, government spending is now vastly higher than before World War II, and the surge in transfer payments financed by distortionary taxation during the 1960s and 1970s emerges as a candidate to explain part of the subsequent growth slowdown. In comparative terms, the UK has been less

Table 18 **Government expenditures as percentages of GDP, 1870–1999**

	1870	1913	1937	1960	1980	1999
Total outlays						
Australia	18.3	16.5	14.8	21.2	31.6	31.8
Belgium*	n/a	13.8	21.8	30.3	58.6	47.9
France	12.6	17.0	29.0	34.6	46.1	52.1
Germany	na	14.8	34.1	32.4	47.9	45.9
Italy*	11.9	11.1	24.5	30.1	41.9	48.3
Japan	n/a	8.3	25.4	17.5	32.0	38.1
Netherlands*	9.1	9.0	19.0	33.7	55.2	42.7
Norway	5.9	9.3	11.8	29.9	37.5	46.2
Sweden	5.7	10.4	16.5	31.0	60.1	56.0
UK	9.4	12.7	30.0	32.2	43.0	39.1
USA	7.3	7.5	19.7	27.0	31.8	30.0

	1880	1910	1930	1960	1980	1995
Social transfers						
Australia	0.0	1.1	2.1	7.4	12.8	17.7
Belgium	0.2	0.4	0.6	13.1	30.4	31.7
France	0.5	0.8	1.1	13.4	22.6	30.2
Germany	0.5	n/a	5.0	18.1	25.7	24.8
Italy	0.0	0.0	0.1	13.1	21.2	25.3
Japan	0.1	0.2	0.2	4.0	11.9	18.3
Netherlands	0.3	0.4	1.2	11.7	28.3	31.8
Norway	1.1	1.2	2.4	7.9	21.0	23.4
Sweden	0.7	1.0	2.6	10.8	25.9	29.6
UK	0.9	1.4	2.6	10.2	16.4	21.4
USA	0.3	0.6	0.6	7.3	15.0	19.5

Sources: Total outlays from Tanzi and Schuknecht (1997), updated using OECD (2000a); social transfers, defined to include spending on pensions, welfare, unemployment benefits and health, from Lindert (1994, 1996), updated using Roseveare *et al.* (1996).
* Central government only until 1937.

prone to these developments than has the average European country. Table 19 reports a rise of 5.2 percentage points in the share of distortionary taxes in GDP since 1955 compared with an average in other European countries of 13.5 percentage points.

Table 19 **Distortionary tax revenues (% GDP)**

	1955	1980	1998
Australia	14.9	21.5	22.3
Austria	19.5	28.9	31.4
Belgium	15.3	33.0	34.0
Canada	13.5	24.9	28.0
Denmark	15.0	29.0	33.1
Finland	15.2	20.5	31.8
France			31.2
Germany	20.2	27.6	26.7
Greece			19.8
Ireland	11.8	21.3	19.6
Italy	17.1	22.0	28.5
Japan	11.4	22.3	23.0
Netherlands	17.9	35.6	29.0
New Zealand	20.2	25.0	22.5
Norway	15.8	30.9	27.4
Portugal	9.3	18.0	19.6
Spain			23.8
Sweden	18.2	38.5	40.5
Switzerland	12.9	24.9	28.7
UK	19.6	26.2	24.8
USA	19.1	26.3	24.3

Sources: OECD (1981, 2000d).

Although there has been no dramatic fall in total government outlays relative to GDP in the last twenty years, there has been a switch from direct to indirect taxation, and in 1980 benefits, including pensions, were decoupled from earnings and linked instead to prices, which implied a saving by the mid-1990s of about 3 per cent of GDP (Tyrie, 1996). Using the equations estimated in Kneller *et al.* (1999), we see that these reforms to fiscal policy taken together would be predicted to raise the growth rate by 0.5 per cent per year or more. Indeed, following this line of argument, the timidity of the Conservatives in backing away from radical welfare reform and in failing to widen the VAT base – which is quite narrow by European standards (Owens and Whitehouse, 1996) – would seem disappointing.

Here, however, we reach a point at which appraisal becomes very difficult. In particular, it is important to recognise that pursuing faster growth by these means has had consequences for the distribution of income. The Gini coefficient of income inequality rose by around 8 percentage points in the late 1980s and early 1990s, and this seems to have resulted primarily from the squeeze on benefits and the change in the structure of taxation noted above as potentially good for growth (Atkinson, 1999: 70). Whether this has been worthwhile or should have been pushed farther is a matter of value judgements on which there is no consensus.

Does ICT make a difference?

In the years 1995–2000 there was a remarkable upturn in productivity growth in the United States, which had been quite anaemic for the previous twenty years or so. For the first time since 1950 European catch-up ceased and productivity gaps between the US and Europe started to increase again – including that with the UK. This development obviously owed a good deal to the impact of ICT, and the Solow Productivity Paradox (that you could see the computer age everywhere but in the productivity statistics) seemed well and truly exploded. This episode raises a number of questions, including:

- How does the impact of ICT in the UK compare with that in the USA?
- Does the ICT revolution imply that the UK productivity gap with the USA is set to widen?

• Is ICT likely to improve British productivity performance
  relative to that of other European countries?

An important point to note is that ICT poses problems for the
measurement of real GDP because the (quality adjusted) prices of
ICT equipment have fallen dramatically and many of the international and intertemporal comparisons currently available are sen-
sitive to the different procedures adopted by national statistical
offices to deal with this. Oulton (2001) estimates that if the UK
measured on the (more accurate) American basis, this would add
about 0.15 per cent per year to GDP growth in the 1979–89 period
and 0.3 per cent per year in 1989–98. However, it would also increase the growth rate of inputs because measured growth of the
capital stock would rise by 1.22 (1.63) per cent per year in the former (latter) period, such that the impact on TFP growth would be
negligible.

Table 20 (on page 96) offers a growth accounting perspective
on the role of ICT in labour productivity growth in the UK and the
USA. As noted in Chapter 3, the contribution of a new technology
comes both from the introduction of a new type of capital and its
impact on TFP growth. In the case of ICT, this can come from
technological progress in ICT production and disembodied
spillover effects in the rest of the economy. The impact of ICT
capital deepening depends on the weight (factor share) that ICT
capital has in the economy, which was obviously very small in the
early days of the technology but has risen over time.

Table 20 reports a big increase in the contribution of ICT to
American growth in the second half of the 1990s, both from the
use of ICT capital and, to a lesser extent, from technological
progress in ICT production. The extra contribution from capital

Table 20 **The contribution of ICT to labour productivity growth (% per year)**

	USA			UK		
	1974–90	1991–5	1996–2000	1979–89	1990–4	1994–8
Output/Hour Growth	1.36	1.54	2.78	2.25	2.66	1.66
Output Growth	3.06	2.75	5.03	2.52	1.44	3.17
ICT Capital	0.42	0.48	1.14	0.40	0.49	0.72
TFP in ICT Production	0.17	0.24	0.50		0.30	0.66
Other Capital	0.34	0.03	0.01	0.52	0.96	0.11
Other TFP	0.42	0.79	1.13	1.32	0.93	0.19
Memorandum item						
ICT Income/GDP (%)	3.3	5.3	6.3	1.4	2.2	3.6

Sources: US: estimates based on Oliner and Sichel (2000), as updated in Sichel (2001); UK: estimates for ICT capital and GDP adjusted for ICT measured as in USA from Oulton (2001); TFP growth in ICT production based on unpublished IMF estimates for 1991–6 and 1997–9. TFP includes labour quality.

deepening was largely due to the rising weight of ICT capital. The USA also enjoyed a large increase in TFP growth outside of ICT production; this accounted for 1.13 per cent per year in 1996–2000 compared with 0.59 per cent in 1974–90. An examination of patterns of sectoral productivity growth suggests that this certainly owed something to spillovers from ICT (Stiroh, 2001), but quite how much is debatable since business cycle effects may play a large part (Gordon, 2000).

The contribution of ICT capital deepening in the UK appears to have nearly matched that in the USA until the mid-1990s, and the recent shortfall comes mostly from a lower weight for ICT capital rather than a slower growth in ICT capital per hour worked. The estimates in Table 17 showed that the labour productivity gap in 1999 owed less to ICT capital than is often supposed. The contribution of TFP growth in ICT production also appears to have been quite similar in both economies. The other big difference between the UK and the USA in the last five years has been in the rate of TFP growth outside the ICT production sector.

The future for the productivity gap with the USA depends on two things. First, whether the productivity surge in the late 1990s in the USA was mainly due to cyclical factors, in which case there will be a period of slower growth in the USA in which excessive investment in ICT capital is corrected. Second, whether, with a lag, the UK is about to follow the USA in enjoying a higher impact from ICT as the share of ICT capital rises and productivity spillovers build up. If both these turn out to be the case, the *status quo* before the mid-1990s will be resumed; if neither, then a new phase of relative economic decline vis-à-vis the United States will occur. Since there is no reason to believe that lack of technological congruence will play a part, this would result from weak social capability.

The evidence strongly suggests that productivity gains from ICT depend on the ability effectively to implement organisational change as well as invest in ICT capital (Brynjolfsson and Hitt, 2000). This is exactly where the British economy of 25 years ago would have been at a huge disadvantage, given its lethal cocktail of weak competition, pervasive agency problems and deleterious industrial relations. In that sense ICT provides an excellent test of the success of the post-1979 reforms. In fact, the UK appears by the mid-1990s to have developed to a relatively high degree the flexibility of working practices that the ICT literature believes is required to take advantage of the opportunities that the new technology offers. The survey evidence reported in OECD (1999b) showed that Britain was second only to Sweden in this regard, and well ahead of both France and Germany.

On the other hand, educational standards still lag well behind the best in Europe in terms of preparation at the level needed to participate effectively in the knowledge economy. In tests conducted by the OECD in the mid-1990s only 49 per cent of the working-age group had this level of achievement compared with 74 per cent in the top country, Sweden (OECD, 2000c).

It is also worth considering barriers to entrepreneurship, since business start-ups matter for the effective exploitation of the opportunities presented by ICT. Here there is some encouraging news but also a possible cloud on the horizon. Nicoletti *et al.* (2000) found that the legacy of the Conservative years was that the UK had the lowest regulatory burdens on business and the second least onerous employment legislation (after the USA) of the 21 OECD countries in their survey of conditions in 1998. On virtually the same day that paper was published, however, the *Financial Times* ran a story in which red tape introduced by the new Labour government was estimated to have cost business £10 billion and was claimed by business leaders to be strangling the entrepreneurial spirit (Brown, 2000).

How have things worked out so far? Comparing Britain with the rest of Europe, the early evidence from growth accounting is mildly encouraging. A recent paper by Colecchia (2001) has reported that the contribution of ICT capital to growth was 0.29, 0.32 and 0.36 per cent per year respectively in Germany, France and Italy. This appears to be distinctly lower than in the UK, although the estimates are not directly comparable with those in Table 20, and reinforces the point made in Table 17 that ICT capital does not seem to explain labour productivity gaps with France and Germany.

Concluding comments

Broadly speaking the evidence suggests that changes in policy and institutions should have been favourable for growth. The productivity growth record of the 1990s has been rather mixed, however, and at this point it is reasonable to say that relative economic decline in comparison with Europe may have ceased but it has not been definitely reversed. This outcome is a good deal better than might have been expected in 1979. Nevertheless, further reforms and/or a long period of macroeconomic stability may yet be required to make a substantial difference.

The ICT revolution is central to the long-run prognosis since it offers the prospect of a period of faster growth and requires substantial managerial effort to achieve the potential productivity pay-off. This is exactly the type of challenge that British firms failed to meet in the Golden Age. Early signs have been reasonably encouraging, even though the UK was outpaced by the USA in the late twentieth century.

The Labour government has effectively rejected the supply-side policies of its 1970s predecessors and promises a programme of microeconomic reform aimed at correcting market failures that impair productivity performance (HM Treasury, 2000). This would be a big improvement; it is to be hoped that government failure does not get in the way.

6 CONCLUSIONS

The foregoing chapters contain a good deal of careful argument accompanied by an unrelenting array of detailed tables. For those with little time and/or inclination for statistics, who are prepared to take things on trust, the following are brief and rather crude summary points of what those chapters contain.

1   The long-run British experience has been one of relative economic decline with economic growth below that elsewhere. Real GDP per person was almost six times the 1870 level in 1999, but the UK has slipped from the second-highest level in 1870 to seventeenth in 1999.

2   Since 1979, relative decline against OECD countries has largely ceased. Nevertheless, at the end of the twentieth century there was still a substantial labour productivity gap with peer group countries such as Germany and the United States. This was largely explained by physical and human capital per hour worked in the former case and by physical capital and R & D per hour worked in the latter case.

3   The story is certainly not one of absolute decline, even if measures of economic welfare broader than GDP are considered. On the contrary, the large gains in life expectancy and reductions in time spent in market work during the twentieth century imply that living standards grew much more rapidly than

is reflected in the national accounts.

4   The early postwar years were a Golden Age of economic growth in Europe. At this point, the UK grew faster than ever before or since, but less than other European economies. The present growth potential of the economy is, however, well above that of the late nineteenth century or even the period of the Industrial Revolution.

5   The most serious British failures are to be found in the 1950s until the 1970s. Before World War II our inability to keep up with the United States was largely unavoidable and was shared by the rest of Europe. The interventionist policies and out-moded institutions of early postwar Britain were costly in an era of strong growth opportunities. This period saw both market and government failures.

6   Relative economic decline has resulted from weak productivity performance rather than simply from low investment. A relatively weak capacity for innovation and for making effective use of technological change have been at the heart of disappointing British growth. This reflects weakness of competition and managerial failure in firms which went largely unchecked by their owners.

7   Given the prevalence of these agency costs in British firms, for much of the twentieth century governments were seriously mistaken in seeking to improve productivity outcomes through industrial rather than competition policy. The reforms pursued by the Conservatives after 1979 and largely accepted subsequently by New Labour have improved the incentive structures facing firms and workers and imply that growth performance has been better than would have been expected under a continuation of the policies of the 1970s.

REFERENCES

Abramovitz, M. (1993), 'The Search for the Sources of Growth:
   Areas of Ignorance, Old and New', *Journal of Economic
   History*, 53: 217–43.

Abramovitz, M., and P. David (1996), 'Convergence and Delayed
   Catch-Up: Productivity Leadership and the Waning of
   American Exceptionalism', in R. Landau, T. Taylor and G.
   Wright (eds), *The Mosaic of Economic Growth*, Stanford
   University Press, Stanford: 21–62.

Adams, W. J. (1989), *Restructuring the French Economy*, Brookings,
   Washington.

Aghion, P., M. Dewatripont, and P. Rey (1997), 'Corporate
   Governance, Competition Policy and Industrial Policy',
   European Economic Review, 41: 797–805.

Aldcroft, D. H., and H. W. Richardson (1969), *The British
   Economy, 1870–1939*, Macmillan, London.

Alford, B. W. E. (1996), *Britain in the World Economy since 1880*,
   Longman, London.

Atkinson, A. B. (1999), 'The Distribution of Income in the UK and
   OECD Countries in the Twentieth Century', *Oxford Review of
   Economic Policy*, 15 (4): 56–75.

Bacon, R., and W. Eltis (1996), *Britain's Economic Problem
   Revisited*, Macmillan, London.

Barrell, R., and N. Pain (1997), 'Foreign Direct Investment, Technological Change and Economic Growth within Europe', *Economic Journal*, 107: 1770–86.

Barro, R. J. (1999), 'Notes on Growth Accounting', *Journal of Economic Growth*, 4: 119–37.

Barro, R. J., and J.-W. Lee (2000), 'International Data on Educational Attainment: Updates and Implications', Harvard University Working Paper No. 42, Center for International Development.

Bassanini, A., S. Scarpetta, and P. Hemmings (2001), 'Economic Growth: the Role of Policies and Institutions', OECD Economics Department Working Paper No. 283.

Bean, C. R., and N. F. R. Crafts (1996), 'British Economic Growth since 1945: Relative Economic Decline … and Renaissance?', in N. F. R. Crafts and G. Toniolo (eds), *Economic Growth in Europe since 1945*, Cambridge University Press, Cambridge: 131–72.

Bishop, M., J. Kay, and C. Mayer (1994), 'Introduction: Privatization in Performance', in M. Bishop, J. Kay and C. Mayer (eds), *Privatization and Economic Performance*, Oxford University Press, Oxford: 1–14.

Blomstrom, M., R. E. Lipsey, and M. Zejan (1996), 'Is Fixed Investment the Key to Economic Growth?', *Quarterly Journal of Economics*, 111: 269–76.

Blundell, R., R. Griffith, and J. van Reenen (1999), 'Market Share, Market Value and Innovation in a Panel of British Manufacturing Firms', *Review of Economic Studies*, 66: 529–54.

Booth, A. (1987), 'Britain in the 1930s: a Managed Economy?', *Economic History Review*, 40: 499–522.

Bowden, S., J. Foreman-Peck, and T. Richardson (2001), 'The

Postwar Productivity Failure: Insights from Oxford (Cowley)',
Business History, 43: 54–78.

Broadberry, S. N. (1997), 'Forging Ahead, Falling Behind and
Catching-Up: a Sectoral Analysis of Anglo-American
Productivity Differences, 1870–1910', *Research in Economic
History*, 17: 1–37.

Broadberry, S. N. (1998), 'How Did the United States and
Germany Overtake Britain? A Sectoral Analysis of
Comparative Productivity Levels, 1870–1990', *Journal of
Economic History*, 58: 375–407.

Broadberry, S. N. (2002), 'Human Capital and Productivity
Performance: Britain, the United States and Germany,
1870–1990', in P. David, P. Solar and M. Thomas (eds),
Economic Challenges of the 21st Century in Historical Perspective,
Oxford University Press, Oxford.

Broadberry, S. N., and N. F. R. Crafts (1992), 'Britain's
Productivity Gap in the 1930s: Some Neglected Factors',
Journal of Economic History, 52: 531–58.

Broadberry, S. N., and N. F. R. Crafts (1996), 'British Economic
Policy and Industrial Performance in the Early Postwar
Period', *Business History*, 38: 65–91.

Broadberry, S. N., and N. F. R. Crafts (2001), 'Competition and
Innovation in 1950s Britain', *Business History*, 43: 97–118.

Broadberry, S. N., and S. Ghosal (2000), 'Explaining
Comparative Productivity Levels in Services', mimeo,
University of Warwick.

Broadberry, S. N., and A. Marrison (2002), 'External Economies
of Scale in the Lancashire Cotton Industry, 1900–1950',
Economic History Review, 55: 51–77.

Broadberry, S. N., and K. Wagner (1996), 'Human Capital and

Productivity in Manufacturing during the Twentieth Century: Britain, Germany and the United States', in B. van Ark and N. F. R. Crafts (eds), *Quantitative Aspects of Postwar European Economic Growth*, Cambridge University Press, Cambridge: 244–70.

Brown, K. (2000), 'Entrepreneurs Attempting to Unravel Jungle of Red Tape', *Financial Times*, 8 May.

Brynjolfsson, E., and L. M. Hitt (2000), 'Beyond Computation: Information Technology, Organizational Transformation and Business Performance', *Journal of Economic Perspectives*, 14 (4): 23–48.

Central Statistical Office (1992), *Monthly Review of External Trade Statistics: Annual Supplement*, HMSO, London.

Coates, D. (1994), *The Question of UK Decline*, Harvester Wheatsheaf, London.

Colecchia, A. (2001), 'The Impact of Information and Communications Technology on Growth', OECD STI Working Paper.

Crafts, N. F. R. (1989), 'Revealed Comparative Advantage in Manufacturing, 1899–1950', *Journal of European Economic History*, 18: 127–37.

Crafts, N. F. R. (1995), 'The Golden Age of Economic Growth in Western Europe, 1950–1973', *Economic History Review*, 48: 429–47.

Crafts, N. F. R. (1997), 'The Human Development Index and Changes in Standards of Living: Some Historical Comparisons', *European Review of Economic History*, 1: 299–322.

Crafts, N. F. R. (1998), 'Forging Ahead and Falling Behind: The Rise and Relative Decline of the First Industrial Nation', *Journal of Economic Perspectives*, 12 (2): 193–210.

Crafts, N. F. R. (1999), 'East Asian Growth Before and After the Crisis', *IMF Staff Papers*, 46: 139–66.

Crafts, N. F. R. (2001), 'The Contribution of Increased Life Expectancy to Growth of Living Standards, 1870–1998', mimeo, London School of Economics.

Crafts, N. F. R. (2002), 'UK Real National Income, 1950–1998: Some Grounds for Optimism', *National Institute Economic Review*, 181, forthcoming.

Crafts, N. F. R., and M. O'Mahony (2001), 'A Perspective on UK Productivity Performance', *Fiscal Studies*, 22: 271–306.

Crafts, N. F. R., and M. Thomas (1986), 'Comparative Advantage in UK Manufacturing Trade, 1910–1935', *Economic Journal*, 96: 629–45.

Crafts, N. F. R., and A. J. Venables (2001), 'Globalization and Geography: an Historical Perspective', Centre for Economic Policy Research Discussion Paper No. 3079.

Cragg, M. I., and I. J. A. Dyck (1999), 'Management Control and Privatization in the UK', *Rand Journal of Economics*, 30: 475–97.

Crouch, C. (1993), *Industrial Relations and European State Traditions*, Clarendon Press, Oxford.

Denison, E. F. (1967), *Why Growth Rates Differ*, Brookings, Washington.

Denny, K., and S. Nickell (1992), 'Unions and Investment in British Industry', *Economic Journal*, 102: 874–87.

Disney, R., J. Haskel, and Y. Heden (2000), 'Restructuring and Productivity Growth in UK Manufacturing', Centre for Economic Policy Research Discussion Paper No. 2463.

Edelstein, M. (1976), 'Realized Rates of Return on UK Home and Foreign Investment in the Age of High Imperialism', *Explorations in Economic History*, 13: 283–329.

Edgerton, D. E. H. (1996), *Science, Technology and the British Industrial 'Decline'*, Cambridge University Press, Cambridge.

Edgerton, D. E. H., and S. Horrocks (1994), 'British Industrial Research and Development before 1945', *Economic History Review*, 47: 213–38.

Edwards, J. R. (1989), *A History of Financial Accounting*, Routledge, London.

Eichengreen, B. (1996), 'Institutions and Economic Growth: Europe after World War II', in N. F. R. Crafts and G. Toniolo (eds), *Economic Growth in Europe since 1945*, Cambridge University Press, Cambridge: 38–72.

Elbaum, B., and W. Lazonick (1986), 'An Institutional Perspective on British Decline', in B. Elbaum and W. Lazonick (eds), *The Decline of the British Economy*, Clarendon Press, Oxford.

Elliott, D. C., and J. D. Gribbin (1977), 'The Abolition of Cartels and Structural Change in the UK', in A. P. Jacquemin and H. W. de Jong (eds), *Welfare Aspects of Industrial Markets*, Nijhoff, Leiden: 345–65.

Ergas, H. (1987), 'Does Technology Policy Matter?', in B. R. Guile and H. Brooks (eds), *Technology and Global Industry*, National Academy Press, Washington: 191–245.

Europe Economics (1998), *Water and Sewage Industries: General Efficiency and Potential for Improvement*, Ofwat, Birmingham.

Foreman-Peck, J. (1990), 'The 1856 Companies Act and the Birth and Death of Firms', in P. Jobert and M. Moss (eds), *The Birth and Death of Companies: an Historical Perspective*, Parthenon Publishing Group, Carnforth: 33–46.

Gardner, N. (1976), 'The Economics of Launching Aid', in A. Whiting (ed.), *The Economics of Industrial Subsidies*, HMSO, London.

Geroski, P. (1990), 'Innovation, Technological Opportunity and Market Structure', *Oxford Economic Papers*, 42: 586–602.

Gordon, R. J. (2000), 'Does the New Economy Measure Up to the Great Inventions of the Past?', *Journal of Economic Perspectives*, 14 (4): 49–74.

Gourvish, T. R. (1987), 'British Business and the Transition to a Corporate Economy: Entrepreneurship and Management Structures', *Business History*, 29: 18–45.

Greenaway, D., and C. Milner (1994), 'Determinants of the Inter-Industry Structure of Protection in the UK', *Oxford Bulletin of Economics and Statistics*, 56: 399–419.

Greenhalgh, C. (1990), 'Innovation and Trade Performance in the United Kingdom', *Economic Journal*, 100: 105–18.

Hannah, L. (1974), 'Takeover Bids in Britain before 1950: An Exercise in Business Pre-History', *Business History*, 16: 65–77.

Hannah, L. (1983), *The Rise of the Corporate Economy*, Methuen, London.

Haskel, J. (1991), 'Imperfect Competition, Work Practices and Productivity Growth', *Oxford Bulletin of Economics and Statistics*, 53: 265–79.

HM Treasury (2000), *Productivity in the UK: the Evidence and the Government's Approach*, The Stationery Office, London.

Jackson, T., N. Marks, J. Ralls, and S. Stymne (1997), *Sustainable Economic Welfare in the UK, 1950–1996*, Centre for Environmental Strategy, University of Surrey, Guildford.

Kennedy, W. P. (1987), *Industrial Structure, Capital Markets and the Origins of British Economic Decline*, Cambridge University Press, Cambridge.

Kneller, R., M. F. Bleaney, and N. Gemmell (1999), 'Fiscal Policy and Growth: Evidence from OECD Countries', *Journal of*

Public Economics, 74: 171–90.

Kormendi, R. C., and P. C. Meguire (1985), 'Macroeconomic Determinants of Growth', *Journal of Monetary Economics*, 16: 141–63.

Landes, D. S. (1969), *The Unbound Prometheus*, Cambridge University Press, Cambridge.

Landes, D. S. (1998), *The Wealth and Poverty of Nations*, Little, Brown, London.

Leunig, T. C. (2001), 'New Answers to Old Questions: Explaining the Slow Adoption of Ring Spinning in Lancashire, 1880–1913', *Journal of Economic History*, 61: 439–66.

Lewchuk, W. (1989), 'Fordist Technology and Britain: the Diffusion of Labor Speed-Up', University of Warwick Economic Research Paper No. 340.

Lewis, F. D. (1979), 'Explaining the Shift of Labor from Agriculture to Industry in the United States 1869 to 1899', *Journal of Economic History*, 39: 681–98.

Lindert, P. H. (1994), 'The Rise of Social Spending, 1880–1930', *Explorations in Economic History*, 31: 1–37.

Lindert, P. H. (1996), 'What Limits Social Spending?', *Explorations in Economic History*, 33; 1–34.

Maddison, A. (1989), *The World Economy in the Twentieth Century*, OECD, Paris.

Maddison, A. (1991), *Dynamic Forces in Capitalist Development*, Oxford University Press, Oxford.

Maddison, A. (1995), *Monitoring the World Economy, 1820–1992*, OECD, Paris.

Maddison, A. (1996), 'Macroeconomic Accounts for European Countries', in B. van Ark and N. F. R. Crafts (eds), *Quantitative Aspects of Postwar European Economic Growth*,

Cambridge University Press, Cambridge: 27–83.

Maddison, A. (2001), *The World Economy: A Millennial Perspective*, OECD, Paris.

Maizels, A. (1963), *Industrial Growth and World Trade*, Cambridge University Press, Cambridge.

Matthews, R. C. O., C. H. Feinstein and J. C. Odling-Smee (1982), *British Economic Growth, 1856–1973*, Stanford University Press, Stanford.

McCloskey, D. N. (1970), 'Did Victorian Britain Fail?', *Economic History Review*, 23: 446–59.

Meeks, G. (1977), *Disappointing Marriage*, Cambridge University Press, Cambridge.

Metcalf, D. (1994), 'Transformation of British Industrial Relations? Institutions, Conduct and Outcomes, 1980–1990', in R. Barrell (ed.), *The UK Labour Market*, Cambridge University Press, Cambridge: 126–57.

Michie, R. C. (1988), 'The Finance of Innovation in Late Victorian and Edwardian Britain: Possibilities and Constraints', *Journal of European Economic History*, 17: 491–530.

Middleton, R. (1996), *Government Versus the Market*, Edward Elgar, Cheltenham.

Middleton, R. (2000), *The British Economy since 1945*, Macmillan, London.

Miller, T. R. (2000), 'Variations between Countries in Values of Statistical Life', *Journal of Transport Economics and Policy*, 34: 169–88.

Millward, R. (1997), 'The 1940s Nationalizations in Britain: Means to an End or the Means of Production', *Economic History Review*, 50: 209–34.

Mitchell, B. R. (1988), *British Historical Statistics*, Cambridge

University Press, Cambridge.

Morris, D. J., and D. Stout (1985), 'Industrial Policy', in D. J. Morris (ed.), *The Economic System in the UK*, Oxford University Press, Oxford: 851–94.

Murray, C. J. L. (1996), 'Rethinking DALYs', in C. J. L. Murray and A. D. Lopez (eds), *The Global Burden of Disease*, Harvard University Press, Cambridge, Mass.: 1–98.

NEDO (1976), *A Study of UK Nationalised Industries*, London.

Nelson, R. R., and G. Wright (1992), 'The Rise and Fall of American Technological Leadership: the Postwar Era in Historical Perspective', *Journal of Economic Literature*, 30: 1931–64.

Newbould, G. D. (1970), *Management and Merger Activity*, Guthstead, Liverpool.

Nickell, S. J. (1996), 'Competition and Corporate Performance', *Journal of Political Economy*, 104: 724–46.

Nickell, S., D. Nicolitsas, and N. Dryden (1997), 'What Makes Firms Perform Well?', *European Economic Review*, 41: 783–96.

Nicoletti, G., S. Scarpetta, and O. Boylaud (2000), 'Summary Indicators of Product Market Regulation with an Extension to Employment Protection Legislation', OECD Economics Department Working Paper No. 226.

Nordhaus, W. D. (1998), 'The Health of Nations: Irving Fisher and the Contribution of Improved Longevity to Living Standards', Cowles Foundation Discussion Paper No. 1200.

Nordhaus, W. D. (2000), 'New Directions in National Economic Accounting', *American Economic Review Papers and Proceedings*, 90: 259–63.

OECD (1981), *Long Term Trends in Tax Revenues of OECD Member Countries*, Paris.

OECD (1999a), *Basic Science and Technology Statistics*, Paris.

OECD (1999b), *Employment Outlook*, Paris.

OECD (2000a), *Economic Outlook*, Paris.

OECD (2000b), *Quarterly National Accounts*, Paris.

OECD (2000c), *Literacy in the Information Age*, Paris.

OECD (2000d), *Revenue Statistics, 1965–1999*, Paris.

Office for National Statistics (2001), *Labour Force Survey*, London.

Oliner, S. D., and D. E. Sichel (2000), 'The Resurgence of Growth in the Late 1990s: Is Information Technology the Story?', *Journal of Economic Perspectives*, 14 (4): 3–22.

O'Mahony, M. (1999), *Britain's Productivity Performance 1950–1996*, NIESR, London.

O'Rourke, K. H., and J. G. Williamson (1994), 'Late Nineteenth Century Anglo-American Factor-Price Convergence: Were Hecksher and Ohlin Right?', *Journal of Economic History*, 54: 892–916.

Oulton, N. (1995), 'Supply-Side Reform and UK Economic Growth: What Happened to the Miracle?', *National Institute Economic Review*, 154: 53–69.

Oulton, N. (1996), 'Workforce Skills and Export Competitiveness', in A. L. Booth and D. J. Snower (eds), *Acquiring Skills*, Cambridge University Press, Cambridge: 201–30.

Oulton, N. (2001), 'ICT and Productivity Growth in the UK', mimeo, Bank of England.

Oulton, N. and G. Young (1996), 'How High is the Social Rate of Return to Investment?', *Oxford Review of Economic Policy*, 12 (2): 48–69.

Owen, G. (1999), *From Empire to Europe*, HarperCollins, London.

Owen, N. (1995), 'Does Britain Have a Comparative Advantage?', mimeo, DTI.

Owens, J., and E. Whitehouse (1996), 'Tax Reform for the 21st Century', *Bulletin for International Fiscal Documentation*, 50: 538–47.

Pavitt, K., and L. Soete (1982), 'International Differences in Economic Growth and the International Location of Innovation', in H. Giersch (ed.), *Emerging Technologies*, Mohr, Tübingen: 105–33.

Pollard, S. (1994), 'Entrepreneurship, 1870–1914', in R. Floud and D. McCloskey (eds), *The Economic History of Britain since 1700*, vol. 2., Cambridge University Press, Cambridge: 62–89.

Prados de la Escocura, L. (1999), 'International Comparisons of Real Product, 1820–1990: An Alternative Data Set', *Explorations in Economic History*, 37: 1–41.

Pratten, C. F., and A. G. Atkinson (1976), 'The Use of Manpower in British Industry', *Department of Employment Gazette*, 84: 571–6.

Republic of China (1999), *Yearbook of Statistics*.

Roseveare, D. W. Leibfritz, D. Fore, and E. Wurzel (1996), 'Ageing Populations, Pension Systems and Government Budgets: Simulations for 20 OECD Countries', OECD Economics Department Working Paper No. 168.

Sanderson, M. (1999), *Education and Economic Decline in Britain, 1870 to the 1990s*, Cambridge University Press, Cambridge.

Scarpetta, S., A. Bassanini, D. Pilat, and P. Schreyer (2000), 'Economic Growth in the OECD Area: Recent Trends at the Aggregate and Sectoral Level', OECD Economics Department Working Paper No. 248.

Schneider, F. (2000), 'The Increase of the Size of the Shadow Economy of 18 OECD Countries: Some Preliminary Explanations', paper presented to Annual Public Choice Meetings, Charleston, South Carolina.

Schneider, F., and D. H. Enste (2000), 'Shadow Economies: Size, Causes, and Consequences', *Journal of Economic Literature*, 38: 77–114.

Sichel, D. E. (2001), 'The Resurgence of Growth in the Late 1990s: an Update and What Lies Ahead?', paper presented to HM Treasury seminar.

Singh, A. (1975), 'Takeovers, Natural Selection and the Theory of the Firm: Evidence from the Postwar UK Experience', *Economic Journal*, 85: 497–515.

Soskice, D. W. (1994), 'Reconciling Markets and Institutions: the German Apprenticeship System', in L. M. Lynch (ed.), *Training and the Private Sector: International Comparisons*, University of Chicago Press, Chicago: 25–60.

Stiroh, K. J. (2001), 'Information Technology and the US Productivity Revival: What Do the Industry Data Say?', Federal Reserve Bank of New York Working Paper No. 115.

Stoneman, P. (1999), 'Government Spending on Research and Development in the UK', *Fiscal Studies*, 20: 223–59.

Tanzi, V. (1969), *The Individual Income Tax and Economic Growth*, Johns Hopkins University Press, Baltimore.

Tanzi, V., and L. Schuknecht (1997), 'Reforming Government: An Overview of Recent Experience', *European Journal of Political Economy*, 13: 395–417.

Taylor, J., and C. Wren (1997), 'Regional Policy: An Evaluation', *Regional Studies*, 31: 835–48.

Thomas, M. (1988), 'Slowdown in the Pre-World War One Economy', *Oxford Review of Economic Policy*, 4 (1): 14–24.

Tyrie, A. (1996), *The Prospects for Public Spending*, Social Market Foundation, London.

United Nations (1999), *International Trade Statistics Yearbook*,

New York.

Usher, D. (1980), *The Measurement of Economic Growth*, Blackwell, Oxford.

van de Klundert, T., and A. van Schaik (1996), 'On the Historical Continuity of the Process of Economic Growth', in B. van Ark and N. F. R. Crafts (eds), *Quantitative Aspects of Postwar European Economic Growth*, Cambridge University Press, Cambridge: 388–414.

Verspagen, B. (1996), 'Technology Indicators and Economic Growth in the European Area: Some Empirical Evidence', in B. van Ark and N. F. R. Crafts (eds), *Quantitative Aspects of Postwar European Economic Growth*, Cambridge University Press, Cambridge: 215–43.

Vickers, J., and G. Yarrow (1988), *Privatization: An Economic Analysis*, MIT Press, Cambridge, Mass.

Vickerstaff, S. (1985), 'Industrial Training in Britain: the Dilemmas of a Corporatist Policy', in A. Cawson (ed.), *Organised Interests and the State*, SAGE Publications, London: 45–64.

Viscusi, W. K. (1993), 'The Value of Risks to Life and Health', *Journal of Economic Literature*, 31: 1912–46.

Wallis, J., and B. Dollery (1999), *Market Failure, Government Failure, Leadership and Public Policy*, Macmillan, London.

World Bank (2001), *World Development Indicators*, Washington, DC.

Wössmann, L. (2000), 'Schooling Resources, Educational Institutions and Student Performance: the International Evidence', Kiel Institute of World Economics Working Paper No. 983.

ABOUT THE IEA

The Institute is a research and educational charity (No. CC 235 351), limited by guarantee. Its mission is to improve understanding of the fundamental institutions of a free society with particular reference to the role of markets in solving economic and social problems.

The IEA achieves its mission by:

- a high-quality publishing programme
- conferences, seminars, lectures and other events
- outreach to school and college students
- brokering media introductions and appearances

The IEA, which was established in 1955 by the late Sir Antony Fisher, is an educational charity, not a political organisation. It is independent of any political party or group and does not carry on activities intended to affect support for any political party or candidate in any election or referendum, or at any other time. It is financed by sales of publications, conference fees and voluntary donations.

In addition to its main series of publications the IEA also publishes a quarterly journal, *Economic Affairs*, and has two specialist programmes – Environment and Technology, and Education.

The IEA is aided in its work by a distinguished international Academic Advisory Council and an eminent panel of Honorary Fellows. Together with other academics, they review prospective IEA publications, their comments being passed on anonymously to authors. All IEA papers are therefore subject to the same rigorous independent refereeing process as used by leading academic journals.

IEA publications enjoy widespread classroom use and course adoptions in schools and universities. They are also sold throughout the world and often translated/reprinted.

Since 1974 the IEA has helped to create a world-wide network of 100 similar institutions in over 70 countries. They are all independent but share the IEA's mission.

Views expressed in the IEA's publications are those of the authors, not those of the Institute (which has no corporate view), its Managing Trustees, Academic Advisory Council members or senior staff.

Members of the Institute's Academic Advisory Council, Honorary Fellows, Trustees and Staff are listed on the following page.

The Institute gratefully acknowledges financial support for its publications programme and other work from a generous benefaction by the late Alec and Beryl Warren.

119

Other papers recently published by the IEA include:

WHO, What and Why?

Transnational Government, Legitimacy and the World Health Organization
Roger Scruton
Occasional Paper 113; ISBN 0 255 36487 3
£8.00

The World Turned Rightside Up

A New Trading Agenda for the Age of Globalisation
John C. Hulsman
Occasional Paper 114; ISBN 0 255 36495 4
£8.00

The Representation of Business in English Literature

Introduced and edited by Arthur Pollard
Readings 53; ISBN 0 255 36491 1
£12.00

A Plea to Economists Who Favour Liberty: Assist the Everyman

Daniel B. Klein

Occasional Paper 118; ISBN 0 255 36501 2

£10.00

Waging the War of Ideas

John Blundell

Occasional Paper 119; ISBN 0 255 36500 4

£10.00

The Changing Fortunes of Economic Liberalism

Yesterday, Today and Tomorrow

David Henderson

Occasional Paper 105 (new edition); ISBN 0 255 36520 9

£12.50

The Global Education Industry

Lessons from Private Education in Developing Countries

James Tooley

Hobart Paper 141 (new edition); ISBN 0 255 36503 9

£12.50

Saving Our Streams

The Role of the Anglers' Conservation Association in
Protecting English and Welsh Rivers
Roger Bate
Research Monograph 53; ISBN 0 255 36494 6
£10.00

Better Off Out?

The Benefits or Costs of EU Membership
Brian Hindley & Martin Howe
Occasional Paper 99 (new edition); ISBN 0 255 36502 0
£10.00

Buckingham at 25

Freeing the Universities from State Control
Edited by James Tooley
Readings 55; ISBN 0 255 36512 8
£15.00

Lectures on Regulatory and Competition Policy

Irwin M. Stelzer
Occasional Paper 120; ISBN 0 255 36511 X
£12.50

Misguided Virtue

False Notions of Corporate Social Responsibility
David Henderson
Hobart Paper 142; ISBN 0 255 36510 1
£12.50

HIV and Aids in Schools

The Political Economy of Pressure Groups and Miseducation
Barrie Craven, Pauline Dixon, Gordon Stewart & James Tooley
Occasional Paper 121; ISBN 0 255 36522 5
£10.00

The Road to Serfdom

The Reader's Digest *condensed version*
Friedrich A. Hayek
Occasional Paper 122; ISBN 0 255 36530 6
£7.50

Bastiat's *The Law*

Introduction by Norman Barry
Occasional Paper 123; ISBN 0 255 36509 8
£7.50

A Globalist Manifesto for Public Policy
Charles Calomiris
Occasional Paper 124; ISBN 0 255 36525 X
£7.50

Euthanasia for Death Duties
Putting Inheritance Tax Out of Its Misery
Barry Bracewell-Milnes
Research Monograph 54; ISBN 0 255 36513 6
£10.00

Liberating the Land
The Case for Private Land-use Planning
Mark Pennington
Hobart Paper 143; ISBN 0 255 36508 X
£10.00

IEA Yearbook of Government Performance 2002/2003
Edited by Peter Warburton
Yearbook 1; ISBN 0 255 36532 2
£15.00

To order copies of currently available IEA papers, or to enquire about availability, please contact:

Lavis Marketing
73 Lime Walk
Oxford OX3 7AD

Tel: 01865 767575
Fax: 01865 750079
Email: orders@lavismarketing.co.uk

The IEA also offers a subscription service to its publications. For a single annual payment, currently £40.00 in the UK, you will receive every title the IEA publishes across the course of a year, invitations to events, and discounts on our extensive back catalogue. For more information, please contact:

Subscriptions
The Institute of Economic Affairs
2 Lord North Street
London SW1P 3LB

Tel: 020 7799 8900
Fax: 020 7799 2137
Website: www.iea.org.uk